Pedagogies of *Deveiling*

Muslim Girls and the *Hijab* Discourse

A Volume in
Critical Constructions: Studies on Education and Society

Series Editor:
Curry Stephenson Malott
West Chester University

Critical Constructions:
Studies on Education and Society

Curry Stephenson Malott, Series Editor

Pedagogies
of *Deveiling*

Muslim Girls and the *Hijab* Discourse

Manal Hamzeh
New Mexico State University

Information Age Publishing, Inc.
Charlotte, North Carolina • www.infoagepub.com

Library of Congress Cataloging-in-Publication Data

Hamzeh, Manal, 1961-
 Pedagogies of *deveiling* : *Muslim* girls and the *Hijab* discourse / Manal
Hamzeh.
   p. cm.
 Includes bibliographical references (p.) and index.
    ISBN 978-1-61735-722-0 (paperback) — ISBN 978-1-61735-723-7 (hardcover) —
ISBN 978-1-61735-724-4 (ebook)
  1. Hijab (Islamic clothing) 2. Muslim women—Clothing. 3. Women in
Islam. I. Title.
  BP190.5.H44H36 2012
  305.48'6970973—dc23

                                                                        2011048229

Cover design by Zeena Hamzeh

Printed in the United States of America

For Taita Susu, Suad Jood (1919–2009),
my grandmother, my first teacher.

Taita, with your intelligence, resiliency, dignity, and love, you instilled in
me your ethics of your *muslimness*, those of justice, compassion,
love of learning, and free will.

To you, Taita, I humbly dedicate this book.

CONTENTS

ACKNOWLEDGMENTS

I labored on this book for more than 5 years thus I am indebted to numerous people, I will be thanking only a few here. First, I extend my gratitude to those *arab-muslim* feminists, who contributed to this work with their groundbreaking theories about Islam and gender. I am especially grateful to Leila Ahmed and Fatima Mernissi.

I am grateful to Layla, Dojua, Abby, and Amy for trusting me with their stories and encouraging me with their intelligence, resiliency, and dignity.

Also, the work that started this book could not have been possible without Dr. Kimberly Oliver who mentored me with utmost support, encouragement, compassion, respect, faith, and love. I am forever grateful to her for the learning opportunities she provided me at different stages of this project.

Coming to the research project then the book would not have become a reality without the most amazing friendship, support, and love of my New Mexican family, Ann Moulton and Robert Moulton. I owe them deep gratitude for their trust in me and faith in my abilities to walk an uncharted road. Also, I would like to thank my loving friend Eileen Raicht-Gray who watched over me with her wisdom, love, and dependable care.

To my friends at New Mexico State University, I am indebted to you all. Particularly, I am thankful for Waded Cruzado and Lisa Bond-Maupin for giving me the chance and for opening an unexpected space in women's studies to make this academic work happen. I am thankful for your compassion, vision, and ethics that kept my eye on gender justice and allowed me as an *arabyyah-muslimah* to work with dignity in a U.S. institution at this time. I would like to also thank Marc Pruyn for believing in my work and helping to give this book a chance. Wholehearted appreciation to my generous friends, Diala Hamaidi and Yousef Arouri, for the numerous conversations they shared with me over dinner in their warm Las Cruces

home. At times of fear, they both taught me how *muslims* are able to negotiate their differences always with love, respect, deep listening, compassion, and sincere friendship.

I am also particularly thankful to Salman Masalha, my friend and poet
in Al Quds. He never hesitated to show me the way into Arabic and Islam.

Also, I owe gratitude to my Hamzeh family. First, I would like to thank
my loving and talented sister, Zeena, who was patient and humorous while
I explained what the book is about. She finally designed the cover of this
book, the first window to my labor. Thank you Zunzoon.

For nurturing my ambitions for social justice, for supporting my risky
endeavors, for loving me unconditionally, and for cheering my optimistic
self in the most difficult times, I am deeply and endlessly grateful to my
amazing and loving parents Rehab Malhas and Zaid Hamzeh.

Finally, I am thankful to Heather Sykes, my partner. Heather read the
manuscript of this book many times and provided me with wise, loving,
encouraging, and respecting feedback. Heather was excited about my
movement and growth throughout the writing process and was bringing
out my *sultanah* self with which I began to imagine some glimpses of pedagogies of *deveiling*. Beyond the specific help and encouragement, I am
grateful to Heather for walking with me through the vulnerabilities of
translations and for crossing with me the many risky borders presented in
my life day in and day out until this book was completed. Heather Sykes
you are my guiding star.

CHAPTER 1

INTRODUCTION

Author's Note: Throughout this book, I alternate between using Muslim and *muslim* as well as Arab and *arab*. The italicized term is used as analytical and political categories useful in "counterhegemonic struggles" but also helpful in acknowledging "the fluidity of cultural expressions, especially of those [*arabs* and/or *muslims*] in the diasporic communities" (Khan, 2002, p. xxii).

Playing in the wilderness of my grandmother's yard, I was riding a big boy's bike, barely reaching the pedals.

Boom. I fell. What happened? I bled in my panties.

My grandmother spotted my blood-marked panties. She was hysterically screaming chanting Qur'anic words while circling her hands around my head.

What is the "fuss" when I frequently fall and walk away with bleeding elbows and knees?

I felt shame, not pain. I had to fight to get to ride that bike in vain. I felt I would not be the same. I was a girl insane. (Manal, age 9)

Pedagogies of Deveiling presents an exploration of a gendering discourse, the *hijab* (veil) discourse, and how it was negotiated by four girls—Layla, Dojua, Abby, and Amy[1] who self-identified as Muslims. Given that the noun *hijab* is derived from the Arabic root *hjb*, to hide, guard, prevent, and establish a border or screen (*Lisan Al 'Arab*, a major Arabic dictionary), then the *hijab* is according to *arab-muslim* feminist Fatima Mernissi (1991) multidimensional—visual, spatial, ethical, and spiritual (1991). That is,

Pedagogies of Deveiling: Muslim Girls and the Hijab Discourse,
pp. 1–15

the *hijab* is not only the narrow visual representation of the headscarf some Muslim as well as Christian and Jewish women have been wearing over the centuries in many shapes and forms (Ahmed, 1992), but it is also the spatial *hijab*, the border that challenges Muslim females' mobility in public spaces, the ethical *hijab*, the protector that shelters them from forbiddens, *harams*, like physical/sexual encounters with males, and the spiritual *hijab*, the barrier that prevents them from pursuing deeper knowledge (Mernissi, 1991).

Pedagogies of Deveiling emerged over a period of 3 years while writing up a 14-month long study in which I collaborated with four Muslim girls in two U.S. southwestern border towns—Al Hilal and Al Jiser²—between October 2005 and December 2006. *Pedagogies of Deveiling* stems from the stories of these four Muslim girls woven with my stories and perspectives as, مُسلِمة-عَرَبِيّة, *arabyyah-muslimah*³ (the Arabic feminine form of the term Arab-Muslim), the main researcher in the study.

Pedagogies of Deveiling offers an alternative approach to research and pedagogy with *muslim* girls in which the taken-for-granted *hijabs* in the sacred text and their inscriptions on the bodies of these girls are deveiled, or problematized, rethought, questioned, and countered. As such, what *Pedagogies of Deveiling* offers is first critical to *muslim* girls themselves because it shatters the phobia and the impossibility of reinterpreting some canonical Islamic sacred texts in relation to the *hijabs* and gender. These androcentric interpretations have been monopolized by the male elite (Ahmed, 1992; Mernissi, 1991) and have socially constructed a gendering discourse for centuries.

What *Pedagogies of Deveiling* puts forward is also critical to educational researchers and teachers who have reduced a central gendering discourse in the lives of *muslim* girls to a headscarf. They have regarded the headscarf as culturally determined and not possible to challenge especially by the girls themselves. This book suggests an alternative understanding of the very disregarded and underexposed *hijab* discourse in the lives of *muslim* girls. With this understanding, it offers ways of doing collaborative work with/among Muslim young people. That is, with the willingness to continuously deconstruct the *hijabs*; scholars and teachers may rethink how to work with *muslim* girls as agents of change countering the *hijab* discourse that is central in their lives and is in tension with the myriad competing normative discourses of this time. It is with the understanding of the *hijabs* as a gendering discourse; scholars and teachers may rethink how to work with *muslim* girls as collaborators in education and agents able to create their own possibilities of social/gender justice.

Finally, *Pedagogies of Deveiling* offers a vision for how the sacred text reinterpreted by critical feminist epistemologies may represent a curriculum that is open to critique and holds potential for change toward justice.

THEORETICAL FRAMEWORK

The justification and the theoretical framing of *Pedagogies of Deveiling* were an interaction between, (1) my girlhood experiences, as *arabyyah-muslimah*, researcher and educator, (2) *arab-muslim* and postcolonial feminists, (3) poststructural feminists bodily discourses, and (4) current educational studies on/about Muslim girls.

Girlhood Experiences of an *arabyyah-muslimah*

To conceptualize the study, as an *arabyyah-muslimah*, I reflected on the centrality of the *hijab* discourse throughout my life and its implication on my ambitions specifically for physical activity opportunities and more generally for wider educational opportunities. At the early stages of designing the study and digging into my forgotten pedagogical memories, I began to journal stories of my girlhood playing in the streets, excelling as an athlete, and dressing up especially in public. Quickly, I became aware that the three *hijabs*, in their visual, spatial and ethical forms, were present in my life and have a strongly influenced my pedagogical journey.

As a young girl, throughout the 1960-1970s, I lived in *arab-muslim* context. I lived in the Hashemite Kingdom of Jordan, a country with a neocolonial, hyperpatriarchal, and undemocratic regime, and an *arab-muslim* majority population. In this context, I was constantly challenged to negotiate complex and intersecting hegemonic discourses. However, it seemed that the *hijab* discourse was the most powerful discourse challenging my way of dress, as an athlete, and my movement in public. It was the biggest challenge to my wider educational opportunities as a girl.

Most of my childhood, I was around my maternal grandmother. She was particularly the more-pious family member and the only one explicitly telling me how I had to cover and protect my body as girl. One day when I was playing in her yard and I was riding a big boy's bike barely reaching the pedals, I fell. I was 9 at the time. When she spotted my blood-marked panties, she was hysterically screaming and chanting Qur'anic verses. I recall my anger and confusion about her panic and her severe prohibition not allowing me to bike again.

Preparing for the study in this book, I realized that this incident was the beginning of my fight with the gender constructions inscribed on my body as a girl and its association with the Qur'an and my *muslimness*. I wrote in my journal (April 2005),

What is the "fuss" when I frequently fall and walk away with bleeding elbows and knees? I felt shame, not pain. I had to fight to get to ride that bike in vain. I felt I would not be the same. I was a girl insane.

Approaching my teen years and becoming more physically active, the messages limiting my body as a girl were contradictory and not as blunt as the ones my grandmother continuously conveyed to me. Most of the time, my parents and my teachers were encouraging me to take advantage of any learning or fun opportunity overtly open for boys. However, at the same time, the messages from the larger society were putting limits on my body different than those set on my older brother or on boys in general. In high school and after 2 years of winning national awards playing on the school's and national basketball and handball teams, right before going to college, I was shocked to know that the athletic scholarships in the University of Jordan were exclusively for boys. My male peers were granted these scholarships automatically, though most of them were not as good athletes as I was or did not have as good academic profiles and ambitions as their female peers. This was another junction in my life when I realized the hidden rules in my *arab-muslim* homeland were constructed to privilege the boys and not to open the doors of education for me as girl.

With my dormant hurtful thoughts and shameful girlhood stories surfacing, I found myself interested in listening to *muslim* girls' stories "close up and large" (Greene, 1995, p. 16). I found myself interested in understanding how the *hijab* discourse came about and how it works in the lives of *muslim* girls now. I found myself interested in working with *muslim* girls to imagine and find "the possibility of looking at things as if they could be otherwise" (Greene, 1995, p. 16). I was interested in discovering how my experiences would help in understanding how *muslim* girls at this time are negotiating the *hijab* discourse in their own lives.

arab-muslim and Postcolonial Feminists

Reading and drawing on the brave and groundbreaking work of several *arab-muslim* feminist scholars like Leila Ahmed (1992), Fatima Mernissi (1991), and Nawal El Saadawi (1998), I developed the conceptual framework of the study. Mainly, I drew on the work of Moroccan sociologist, Fatima Mernissi (1991) who expanded the meanings of the *hijabs* (veils) in Arabic and showed their decontextualized, androcentric interpretations in the primary Islamic texts, the Qur'an and the Hadīth.[4] I also drew on the historicizing work of women's studies in religion scholar,

Leila Ahmed (1992) who historicized the veil and exposed the discourses that constructed gender in Islam.

Particularly, Mernissi's exposure of the multiplicity of the *hijabs* and the circumstances in which they were constructed helped me conceptualize how this gendering discourse became hegemonic. This is what I call the "*hijab* discourse." This discourse had inscribed norms on the bodies of *muslimat, muslim* females, through their dress and mobility and behavior in public; and had been central in their lives for centuries (Ahmed, 1992; Badran, 2009; El Saadawi, 1998; Mernissi, 1991). In Chapter 2, I discuss the main conceptual framework of this study, which details how the *hijab* discourse was constructed and maintained.

I would like to begin by asking the reader to divert attention from the stereotypical colonial media-driven representation of the term *hijab*. I would like to turn the reader away from the superficializing cacophonic debates between the right of a Muslim female to wear a headscarf or the right of the state or the government to demand it be removed or to require that it be worn. The debates are getting louder in the democracies of Europe, Canada, the United States, and Turkey; the theocracies of Iran and Gaza; and the dictatorships of Syria and Sudan. At this time, I ask the reader to stay open to the idea that by utilizing the *hijab* discourse, I am not interested in (re)producing any definitive readings of the *hijabs* to win or lose these dichotomizing debates of "to veil or not veil" the *muslimat*. Moreover, I am not interested in the *hijab* in its one static and popularized representation as the sacred symbol with which some women assert their *muslim* identity. I am not interested in its essentializing representation as the subtext with which neoinvaders justify their occupation and colonization of other nations. Alternatively, I am interested in focusing on a more complex discursive perspective in which intertwined visible and invisible *hijabs* (veils) act as taken-for-granted or godly and sacred values and practices inscribed on the bodies of *muslim* females by normalizing their contribution to public life.

Finally, I drew on the works of critical postcolonial feminist scholars like Sara Ahmed (2002), and Sherene Razack (2008) that complicated the intersectionality of discourses in the lives of *muslims* at this time of empire. I also drew on the works of critical multicultural educators like Nina Asher (2003) and Meetoo and Mirza (2007), who urgently call for practicing critical reflexivity and engaging with difference in an anticolonial and antiracist education. Finally *Pedagogies of Deveiling* draws on the latest work of critical feminist scholars Sirin and Fine (2008) that shows the marvels of working *with muslim* youth to change inequities by using alternative and multiple methods of research.

Poststructural Feminists and Bodily Discourses

Drawing on the works of critical feminist poststructuralist scholars like Judith Butler (1990), Bronwyn Davies (2000), Patti Lather (2007), and Chris Weedon (1999), I conceptualized the *hijab* discourse as one gendering discourse inscribing the bodies of Muslim women. I conceptualize discourse as a "dynamic or network of noncentralized forces" and within a historically contextualized "ideology of dominance" (Bordo, 1993, p. 26). A discourse is also, according to Hesse-Biber and Leavy (2007), "complex interconnected web of modes of being, thinking, and acting ... always located on temporal and spatial axes; thus historically and culturally specific" (p. 82). A dominant, normative, and ideological discourse is constructed through a network of knowledge and language production, with which subjects are materially produced. As such, the body is the site of a discursive production through which its "material and ideological interest" (Shapiro & Shapiro, 2002, p. x) is mediated. Further, the body is "a powerful symbolic form, as surface on which the central rules, hierarchies, and even the metaphysical commitments of a culture are inscribed and thus enforced through the concrete language of the body" (Bordo, 1993, p. 165).

In the case of a gendering discourse, the female body is constructed and normalized to reassert "existing gender configurations against any attempts to shift or transform power relations" (Bordo, 1993, p. 166). The female body is the site of discipline and an incredibly durable and flexible strategy of social control (Bordo, 1993). The female body as such is rendered as a thing and object representing fixed and essentialized meanings of what *is* a woman and what a woman *can be*. This perspective also acknowledges that a gendering discourse, such as the *hijab* discourse, may separate aspects of a female being from her body and can render the body as absent and away from learning opportunities and from change.

However, the body is not only passively inscribed by a discourse but it is simultaneously a vehicle of the subject's remaking of the world, constantly shifting location, capable of revealing endlessly alternative points of view (Bordo, 1993). In pedagogical terms and to understand young people's bodily experiences and subjectivities in educational contexts, this means that the body is integral to the knowing process, a site of learning as well as resistance (Giroux, 2001). The body is the site of learners' meaning and self-formation and a "visible carrier of self-identity," and thus, can be a crucial site for pedagogical inquiry, critique and possibility (Giroux, 2001). As such the body is fluid and impossible to mold into fixed categories, so it is multiple and changing. The body is not so predictable, and can be the imaginative ground for theorizing around the discursive production of gendered and sexed corporal subjects (Bordo, 1993). In other words, the body of a learner is the medium of inscribed and changing subjectivities as well as an agency of social change.

CURRENT EDUCATIONAL STUDIES

Reviewing, contextualizing, and critiquing the current educational studies, those mainly done *on* Muslim girls, helped develop the pedagogical and ethical justification of this study. To do this task, I drew on the works of poststructural critical feminist scholars like Christine Weedon (1997, 1999) and Hesse-Biber and Leavy (2007), who deconstructed normative discourses and helped us acknowledge neocolonialism, anti-Arab racism, and Islamophobia as the array of discourses intersecting in the lives of *muslim* girls (Razack, 2008; Zine, 2003, 2006a, 2006b, 2007). I have also reviewed the literature of anticolonial, antiracist, and multicultural educational studies and the literature of the specialized area on learning and instruction in physical education. Additionally, to make sense of this literature with my commitment to social justice and equity, I drew on the works of postcolonial critical feminist scholars, like Sara Ahmed (2002), Sherene Razack (2008), and Veena Meetoo and Heidi Safia Mirza (2007), who problematized educational studies that racialize, ethnicize, and culturize Muslims in different transnational and diasporic contexts. I drew on the work of Nina Asher (2003, 2007) who critiqued multicultural educational discourses that address the struggles of diverse students living in the margins of American schools but are still not inviting a dialogue across difference.

Educational Research *on* Muslim Girls

In the past decade and particularly within a very intense and complex post-9/11 social and political context, "Muslim Americans," "Muslim Europeans," and "Muslim immigrants," emerged in the Western popular discourses of "the war on terror" as a dangerous ethnic identity (Sirin & Fine, 2008). According to Sherene Razack (2008), *this Muslim* is a subject of the neoracializing, neo-Orientalist, and neocolonial discourses. It is the subject that is constructed as the devalorized "other," the savage or terrorist, who is dangerous to modernity and to the "project of the empire" (p. 177). This *muslim* is constructed to possess "*cultures* that are inferior and overly patriarchal" (Razack, 2008, p. 171). Moreover, as Edward Said (1979) asserts, these new-empire or neo-Orientalist discourses are constructed by the production of knowledge in certain academic disciplines and maintained by other hegemonizing tools such public relation enterprises, the so-called think tanks, and of course the mainstream coopted media. A byproduct of these new empire or neo-Orientalist discourses is the female *muslim* who needs to be saved from extremely oppressive *muslim* men.

Scholars in Australia, Canada, Europe, New Zealand, Canada, and the United States started to pay attention to *muslim* girls, particularly to those who wear a headscarf in public schools (Elnour & Bashir-Ali, 2003; Hamdan, 2007; Kahan, 2003; Keaton, 2006; Limage, 2000; Meetoo & Mirza, 2007; Sarroub, 2001; Strandbu, 2005; Walseth & Fasting, 2003; Windle, 2004; Zine, 2006a). For example, after the French National Assembly 2004 decision of banning all conspicuous religious symbols in public spaces, Hamdan (2007) and Keaton (2006) claimed that many *muslim* girls wearing headscarves faced the risk of expulsion from public school. Consequently, French *muslim* girls found themselves forced to choose between asserting their ethnic/religious identity through wearing a headscarf and exercising their right to a free education (Hamdan, 2007; Limage, 2000). Both Hamdan (2007) and Keaton (2006) argued that the implication of this ban was an increase in school dropouts among French *muslim* girls. Thus, this ban complicated these girls' struggles in making meaning of their "ethnic-religious" lived realities, and accentuated their difficulties in making perplexing choices between home and school cultures. Likewise, Basit (1997) asserted earlier that Asian-British *muslim* girls receive simultaneous ambiguous messages from their families and the larger British society. They struggled in negotiating both the local Muslim communities' norms of being a *muslim* female and the "stereotypical notions held by some of the teachers, which are apparently based on assumptions regarding the lives of British Muslim girls" (p. 425).

More recently, Zine (2006a), a Muslim feminist scholar, worked in the schools of the greater Toronto area and claimed that *muslim* girls in both secular public schools and gender-segregated Islamic schools struggle to make sense of their identity, gender, and faith living both patriarchal fundamentalism within Muslim communities and secular Islamophobia within mainstream society. Zine describes Islamophobia as "the fear or hatred of Islam and its adherents that translate into individual, ideological and systemic forms of oppression and discrimination" (2006a, p. 239). Accordingly, Muslim girls navigate between their struggles to negotiate the "traditional norms" at home (Zine, 2006a, p. 250) and the racializing hidden curriculum in public schools. Particularly, Zine draws attention to those Muslim girls who wear headscarves and are struggling with their teachers' common assumptions "that they were oppressed at home and that Islam did not value education for women" (2006a, p. 244). These assumptions get translated into the girls' experiences of "low teacher expectations and streaming practices where [they] were encouraged to avoid academic subjects and stick to lower nonacademic streams" (Zine, 2006a, p. 244).

Though these studies have brought *muslim* girls to the center of the anticolonial, antiracist, and multicultural educational studies, educators need to do more in order to understand how *muslim* girls continue to experience challenges to their learning opportunities, particularly in transnational contexts. According to the work of postcolonial feminist scholars like Sara Ahmed (2002), Sherene Razack (2008), and Veena Meetoo and Heidi Safia Mirza (2007), scholars in the above studies are still confronted with the need to explore and understand how Muslims live an array of racializing and ethnicizing discourses which they have to constantly negotiate in transnational and diasporic contexts. Specifically, there is need to understand how *muslims* have to negotiate neocolonialism, anti-Arab racism, and Islamophobia within educational contexts as well as sexism and homophobia within *muslim* communities (Ahmed, 2002; Kugle, 2010; Zine, 2004, 2006a, 2006b).

Moreover, these intersecting hegemonic discourses become more complex to navigate when many *muslim* females live what I call *hijabophobia*, a gendering discourse hidden within Islamophobia. Zine (2006a) refers to this "gendered Islamophobia," as "specific forms of ethno-religious and racialized discrimination leveled at Muslim women" (p. 240). In other words, *hijabophobia* is an underlying sexist/racist discourse within Islamophobia that is complicit in essentializing constructions of *muslim* women and mainly those who are visible with the headscarf they are wearing. Additionally, *hijabophobia* is a discourse that is "historically entrenched within Orientalist representations that cast colonial Muslim women as backward, oppressed victims of misogynist societies" (Zine, 2006a, p. 240). Arguably, this double phobia, though crucial to expose, is limiting many researchers and educators from finding critical ways to counter these constantly changing and interlocking discourses. One, focusing on the exposure of Islamophobia and *hijabophobia* traps researchers and educators in reactionary debates of "to veil or not to veil" (Hamdan, 2007, p. 1) that subtly keep them from going beyond framing the *muslim* girl as *the* problem living with certain racialized norms. Two, it also traps them in tokenistic anti-Islamophobic (Kincheloe, Steinberg, & Stonebanks, 2010) and policy-oriented inclusionary pedagogical approaches (Zine, 2004). Such debates and approaches distract educators and researchers from considering the patriarchal discourses within *muslim* communities that *muslim* girls live day in and day out. In other words, researchers and educators, especially those who are insiders in/to *muslim* contexts, need to critically consider, (1) how *muslim* girls' lived experiences are constituted by the *hijabs* that act as a gendering discourse, and (2) how these girls could practice their agency to counter it along with the other hegemonic discourses in their lives.

Physical Education Studies *About* Muslim Girls

Over the past decade, there have been an increasing number of physical education studies *about muslim* youth, especially *muslim* girls, in the schools of North America, Europe, and Australia. Some of these studies were incited by the literature that claims *muslim* students are increasingly withdrawing from physical education (Benn, 1996, 2000a, 2000b, 2002), facing particular problems when taking physical education (Dagkas & Benn, 2006), and less likely to participate in sports and recreational activities (Cortis, Sawrikar, & Muir, 2007; Hargreaves, 2007) than those students who are not *muslim*.

To date, these scholars have categorized *muslim* students as cultural and linguistic diverse groups (Cortis et al., 2007), religious/faith-based groups (Kahan, 2003; Walseth, 2006; Zaman, 1997), and so-called minorities groups, immigrants or foreigners in the West (De Knop, Theeboom, Wittock, & De Martelaer, 1996; Pfister, 2000; Strandbu, 2005; Walseth & Fasting, 2003). They also group Muslim students with those who are categorized or who identify as Arab (Martin, McCaughtry, & Shen, 2008). As such, Muslim students are either a homogenous group or in the case of Muslim girls they are one monolithic group wearing a headscarf (Kahan, 2003; Walseth & Fasting, 2003; Zaman, 1997). Such reductive and essentializing grouping when used to justify a study actually excludes many Muslim students and overlooks the multiplicities and fluidity of Muslim youth and/or Arab youth. These groupings exclude students who are Muslim but not religious at all. In other words, they exclude those Muslims who are interpreting their *muslimness* in multiple and very private and subtle ways. Additionally, they exclude the Arabs who are not Muslim but are or not living and negotiating dominantly Muslim discourses. Finally, they exclude those Muslim girls who do not wear a headscarf and/or perform their Muslim religiosity or identities in many ways that are often not visible and very much in flux.

Other scholars doing physical education studies *about muslim* youth strategically advocate *for muslim* students and call for "religiously responsive" accommodations in physical education (Elnour & Bashir-Ali, 2003; Kahan, 2003). These scholars attribute *muslim* students' low engagement in physical activity to teachers' misunderstanding of religion and in this case, Islam. They suggest that to include *muslim* students in PE programs, educators need to learn more about Islam in order to accommodate *muslim* norms in dress for girls, body exposure, and physical contact between boys and girls. To the same end, Benn and Dagkas (2006) suggest that in order to include *muslim* students in physical education (PE) and respond to the demands of the religiously accommodating single-sexed PE school programs, university PE teacher training programs must recruit and accommodate *muslim* females adhering to "Islamic requirements." Similarly, Zaman (1997) suggests that physical educators need to provide female exclusive spaces with total screens keeping *muslim* girls away from the gaze of male staff and clients.

Through the above grouping of research participants and suggested accommodations, PE scholars are genuinely seeking to find pedagogical solutions and are calling for adoption of special national policies in order to integrate *muslims* in national sport initiatives and in multicultural physical education curricula and school spaces. Despite these good intentions these same scholars may actually be displacing and excluding more *muslim* students from participating in physical activity. For example, according to Strandbu (2005) religiously responsive accommodations actually end up excluding *muslim* girls from participating in swimming, dancing, competitive athletics, and contact sports. Thus I argue that the above scholars' interest in the inclusion of *muslim* and *arab* students in more physical activities is built on some kind of racial thinking (Razack, 2008) that may be unhelpful in enticing these students' interest in physical activities. According to Sara Ahmed (2002), the *muslims* selected for studies as such come to represent the "strange other" as well as the "culturized and racialized" other (Razack, 2008, p. 171). Razack (2008) argues,

> Although racialized groups are no longer widely portrayed as biologically inferior (as a cruder version of racism would have it), dominant groups often perceive subordinate groups as possessing cultures that are inferior and overly patriarchal, a move described as the culturalization of racism. (p. 173)

Accordingly, I argue that these studies (Benn, 2000a, 2000b, 2002; Cortis, et al., 2007; Dagkas & Benn, 2006; Kahan, 2003; De Knop et al., 1996; Martin et al., 2008; Pfister, 2000; Strandbu, 2005; Walseth, 2006; Walseth & Fasting, 2003; Zaman, 1997) attribute *muslims'* physical inactivity to the confinement of so called "cultural norms" or "Islamic requirements" that end up overemphasizing the hypersexualizing and gendering norms exclusively attributed to *muslims*. While this conceptualization may show educators being responsive to cultural diversity and accordingly acting as promoters of multicultural education, they are actually ranking educational decisions based on the "devalorizing of non-White cultures" (Razack, 2008, p. 173).

Moreover, "culturalization of racism" (Razack, 2008, p. 171) approach to research *on/about muslims* represents norms as rigid values and practices that are fixed and nonnegotiable, and thus, could only be accommodated with best practices or special policies. It also represents norms as values and practices that are recognizable and visible and not as subtle and complicated ways of living *muslimness* in context. For example, besides the visible headscarf or the long cloak that some *muslim* girls wear in public (Elnour & Bashir-Ali, 2003; and Kahan, 2003; Walseth & Fasting, 2003; Zaman, 1997), many other more subtle forms of gendering norms confine *muslim* girls from being physically active such as those serving capitalism in a globalizing and transnational context. These more subtle forms of gendering norms become overlooked when the focus is on what is visually perceived by the researchers as *the* cultural barrier to *muslim* girls' physical activity. That is, these studies (Kahan, 2003; De Knop et al., 1996; Martin et al., 2008; Pfister, 2000; Strandbu, 2005; Walseth, 2006; Walseth & Fasting, 2003; Zaman, 1997) simplify the so-called cultural norms or barriers as isolated reasons theorized out of complex discursive and historical contexts. Such studies also help justify the teachers' reluctance to include *muslim* girls with headscarves when their parents' request that they either be excused from participating in any physical activities or be accommodated with gender segregated spaces. When teachers do not engage *muslim* girls, their parents, and/or authoritative male community leaders, the girls not only end up with limited choices of physical activities but in addition are also not considered as decision makers in their learning process. As such, these racializing studies strip young *muslims* from the possibility of using their agency to negotiate their own *muslimness* in PE and other school spaces.

In contrast to the above studies *on* girls and their physical inactivity, other poststructural feminist scholars have expanded their methodologies and started to work *with* girls. They noted that they are challenged by gender discourses that discourage them from utilizing opportunities for physical activity (Azzarito & Solmon, 2005; Azzarito, Solmon, & Harrison 2006; Flintoff & Scraton, 2001; Oliver & Hamzeh, 2010; Oliver, Hamzeh, & McCaughtry, 2009). For example, working *with* girls in a Mexican-U.S. border town, Oliver and colleagues (2009) called educators who are committed to work *with* girls and finding enjoyable physical activities, to look at the multiplicity and intersectionalities of the discourses of gender, race, and class in schools. They further claim that the intersecting discourses in the lives of girls not only challenge their participation in physical activities, but once identified and critiqued they become possible to interrupt by the girls themselves.

More importantly, while girls may be working to counter the discourses in their lives by becoming physically active they are simultaneously being girly girl (Oliver et al., 2009), being Borderland *meztizas* (Oliver & Hamzeh, 2010), or for that matter, being *muslim* with a headscarf (Hamzeh & Oliver, 2010). While the girls' simultaneous negotiations of several discourses may seem to some scholars and educators contradictory to being physically active it also means that there is a need to understand the locality and the context of the intersecting discourses in the lives of girls and take their lead from the girls themselves in making their own changes to be more physically active (Oliver et al., 2009; Oliver & Hamzeh, 2010). Girls' simultaneous negotiations of several discourses in their lives also justify the need to work *with* the girls as the agents and the creators of their own multiple ways of being physically active. And thus, more studies need to be developed in collaboration *with* girls and more urgently with those who are still approached with racializing studies such as *muslim* girls.

Though the above studies have brought *muslim* girls to the center of the anticolonial, antiracist, physical education, and multicultural educational studies, educators need to do more in order to understand how *muslim* girls continue to experience challenges to their learning opportunities, particularly in transnational contexts. Critical feminist researchers and educators who are committed to working *with muslim* girls, need to find and use alternative pedagogical possibilities that will not trap them in the reactionary debates of "to veil or not to veil" (Hamdan, 2007, p. 1) and the myopic perspective of *muslim* women and girls as those who live their *muslimness* only through a headscarf. Arguably, we need to approach our research in collaboration with all sorts of *muslim* girls and in ways that will enable us to uncover and counter any normative discourse these girls negotiate. Critical feminist researchers and educators still need to listen more carefully, engage, and collaborate with *muslim* girls as agents and counter with them the inequities in their lives including their physical activity needs.

Pedagogies of Deveiling thus emerged from my realization that there is an urgent need to counter the neocolonizing and racializing discourses *on Muslim* females specifically in the educational arena at this time in the so-called West. These discourses were implicating me as a scholar in the very institutions of higher education that produced them and in the field of education in which I was first situated. It became apparent that what I learned in the past few years is worth sharing with a wider audience of student teachers, teachers, parents, policy makers and scholars who are interested in working *with/among young muslims* or are somehow living and learning in proximity with them, and are already paving the way to social justice and equity in education.

THE BOOK'S CHAPTERS

In Chapter 2, "*Deveiling* a Gendering Discourse," I *deveil* how a gendering discourse—that I refer to as the *hijab* discourse—was socially constructed and became central to the lives of all kinds of *muslimat—muslim* women. I expand on the deconstructive analysis of Mernissi (1991) and Clarke (2003) of the canonical texts of *Lisan Al 'Arab* (a major Arabic dictionary), the Qur'an and the Hadīth (the sacred primary and secondary Islamic sources). I then highlight how in the Arabic language and in Islam's fundamental and primary texts, the Qur'an and the Hadīth, the *hijab* is four-dimensional—visual, spatial, ethical, and spiritual (Mernissi, 1991). Thus, the *hijab* discourse as such, is not a simple argument over dress style but it is the unexposed pattern of normative values and practices, which hegemonized the *muslimah's* body in her dress, mobility, and way of life in public, for centuries (Ahmed, 1992; Badran, 2009; El Saadawi, 1998; Mernissi, 1991; Wadud, 1999).

In Chapter 3, "A *Deveiling* Methodology," I map the feminist *deveiling* methodology that guided the study in which I sought to understand how four Muslim girls negotiated the *hijab* discourse in the two southwestern U.S. border towns of Al Hilal and Al Jiser. The methodology was a collaborative project framed by a critical feminist approach to qualitative research in which I used, (1) classical Islamic insider's methods and (2) critical self-reflexivity. These two *deveiling* methods helped me in negotiating the spatial contexts and relationships in the study and consequently interpreting the data.

In Chapter 4, "*Deveiling* Research Access," I analyze in more detail the process of gaining research access into the lives of Layla, Dojua, Abby, and Amy, the four Muslim girls in this study, which became pivotal to the start and continuation of this research project. Specifically, I identify four challenges that emerged in the process of gaining and sustaining access throughout the study duration and they included, (1) being *muslim* enough, (2) *inshallah* (Allah or God willing), (3) being modest enough, and (4) *haram* (forbidden). These challenges were markers of difference on both *muslimness* and the interpretations of the *hijabs* and the *hijab* discourse between the girls, the parents, and myself.

In Chapter 5, "*Deveiling* the *Hijabs*," I discuss how three *hijabs*—visual, spatial, and ethical—acted as a central gendering discourse in the lives of Layla, Dojua, Abby, and Amy, the four Muslim girls who participated in the study. The girls conformed to their parents' particular interpretations of three *hijabs*, in their dress, social activities, and physical activities, and movement in public. They also questioned them and finally deveiled them to cross the fourth spiritual *hijab*. In spaces and moments outside the reach of the *hijab* discourse, the girls renarrated themselves, as *muslim* girls. They called for teachers to pay attention to them with their differences, and, with their similarities to other girls their age in U.S. public schools.

Finally, in Chapter 6, "A Vision of *Deveiling* Pedagogies," I present the implications of this study leading to a vision of *deveiling* pedagogies. I present the lessons and implications of (1) using feminist *ijtihad*, (2) negotiating differences in the process of gaining access (made possible by using my insider's literacies, my fluid insiderness, and building and maintain relationships with key participant) in the lives of these four Muslim girls, and (3) practicing agency to counter the *hijab* discourse. Finally, I share my vision for pedagogies of *deveiling* with those who are interested in working *with/among muslim* girls and their parents. I offer this vision to those who are committed to creating antiracist, anticolonial, antioppressive, and critical multicultural research and educational opportunities.

CHAPTER 2

DEVEILING A GENDERING DISCOURSE

> Reducing or assimilating this concept [the *hijab*] to a scrap of cloth that men have imposed on women to veil them when they go into the street is truly to impoverish this term, not to say to drain it of its meaning, especially when one knows that the *hijab*, according to the Koranic verse [33:53] and al-Tabari's explanation, tafsir, "descended" from Heaven to separate the space between two men. (Mernissi, 1991, p. 95)

In this chapter, I will *deveil* how a gendering discourse, that I refer to as the *hijab* discourse, was socially constructed and became central to the lives of all kinds of *muslimat—muslim* females. To accomplish the task of *deveiling* the *hijab* discourse, I expand on the deconstructive analysis of sociologist Fatima Mernissi (1991) and historian of religion Lynda Clarke (2003) of the canonical texts of *Lisan Al 'Arab* (an Arabic dictionary), the Qur'an and the Hadīth (the sacred primary and secondary Islamic sources). This process of *deveiling* framed the project's methodology, developed the analysis of the data, and lead to my vision of *deveiling* pedagogies.

Before, I begin the thorough process of *deveiling* how the *hijab* discourse was socially constructed; I think it would be helpful to draw the attention of the readers to the linguistic and discursive complexities of the *hijabs*, and thus, differentiate the *hijab* discourse from the superficial and distracting debates over the "scrap of cloth that men have imposed on women" (Mernissi, 1991, p. 95). The noun *hijab* (veil) is based on the Arabic root *hjb*, which means to cover, hide, shelter, protect, and establish a

Pedagogies of Deveiling: Muslim Girls and the Hijab Discourse,
pp. 17–48

barrier, border, screen, or threshold (Mernissi, 1991). In the Arabic language and in Islam's fundamental and primary texts, the Qur'an and the Hadīth, the *hijab* is four-dimensional—visual, spatial, ethical, and spiritual (Mernissi, 1991). That is, the *hijab* is not only the narrow and static visual representation of a headscarf some *muslim* women wear to hide their bodies from the male gaze. It is also the spatial *hijab*, the screen that shelters *muslim* females out of public spaces; the ethical *hijab*, the threshold that protects them from the forbiddens, *harams*, like physical/sexual encounters with males; and the spiritual *hijab*, the cover that blinds one from deeper knowledge (Mernissi, 1991).

Mernissi's (1991) rereadings of the Qur'an and the Hadīth exposed the decontextualized androcentric-popularized meanings of these three *hijabs*. The taken-for-granted meanings of the *hijabs* became complex social normalized codes that hegemonized a gendering discourse. According to poststructural feminists like Hesse-Biber and Leavy (2007) discourse is a "complex interconnected webs of modes of being, thinking, and acting ... they are always located on temporal and spatial axes; thus they are historically and culturally specific" (p. 82). As such, the *hijab* discourse inscribed itself on *muslimat's* bodies through an interconnected set of visible and invisible values and practices that became normalized or taken-for-granted in a specific historical context. Thus the *hijab* discourse as such, is not a simple argument over dress style but it is the unexposed pattern of normative values and practices which act as a "social force that sets the terms for the construction of material 'reality'" (Herschmann, 2004, p. 324) of the *muslimah's* body. These unquestionable normative patterns of values and practices act as noncoercive tools that hegemonize the *muslimah's* body in her dress, mobility, and way of life in public.

Furthermore, the *hijab* discourse is what *arab-muslim* feminists like Leila Ahmed, Nawal El Saadawi, and Fatima Mernissi, as well as *muslim/islamic* feminists like Margot Badran and Amina Wadud, refer to as the "institution" or the hegemonic discourse through which the Muslimah's body became regulated and normalized for centuries (Ahmed, 1992; El Saadawi, 1998; Badran, 2009; Mernissi, 1991; Wadud, 1999).

More important, the *hijab* discourse is *not* about the debates that emerged in particular postcolonial social and political circumstances at the end of the nineteenth century and the beginning of the twentieth century in Algeria and Egypt for example (Ahmed, 1993; Badran, 2009). This *hijab* discourse is not about the debate that Leila Ahmed (1992) calls the "battle of the veil" (p. 145). It is not the controversial political act of Egyptian feminists that Margot Badran calls the "unveiling" (2009, p. 60) movement of Egyptian feminist Huda Sha'rawi in 1923. This *hijab* discourse is not about the debates over the embodiments of a "scrap of cloth" (Mernissi, 1991, p. 95) that first started to widely spread in Muslim/

Islamic countries post 1975 oil boom and particularly post 1979 Iranian Islamic Revolution (Abou El Fadl, 2001; Ahmed, 1992). This discourse is not about the post 9/11 intensifying debate over the constitutionality of a visible religious identity symbol in the public spheres of the "modern democracies" of Europe and North America (Badran, 2009). It is not about the narrow and distracting debates over the issue of "to veil or not to veil" Muslim women for example in global sport events. This *hijab* discourse is not about the reactionary practices of Islamic movements in current neocolonial/colonial contexts such as Afghanistan, Iraq, Jordan, Gaza, Egypt, Sudan et cetera. Nor for that matter, is it a discourse about the blinding debates over the religiosity or piety of *muslim* women wearing a headscarf or not in many Muslim communities all over the world (Mahmood, 2005). Rather, the *hijab* discourse, I am *deveiling* and with which I am framing this book, is the gendering discourse that utilizes *muslim* females' bodies as sites through which their ways of thinking and acting may have been hegemonized and deeply challenged over the centuries (Ahmed, 1992; Badran, 2009; Mernissi, 1991).

In the following, I go beyond the distracting debates over "to veil or not to veil" or beyond the reductive meaning of a "scrap of cloth that men have imposed on women" (Mernissi, 1991, p. 95). I deveil how the *hijab* discourse was socially constructed as a central gendering discourse in the lives of *muslimat* by expanding on Mernissi and Clarke's analysis of the canonical texts. First, I deveil the *hijabs* by (1) deconstructing their reduced linguistic scope in Arabic in the canonical dictionary of *Lisan Al 'Arab* and (2) decontextualizing their popular interpretations in the relevant Qur'anic verses—the primary Islamic sacred text. Second, I (de)authenticate a major popular misogynistic *hadīth*—the secondary Islamic sacred text. Both Mernissi and Clarke worked directly with *the* text that became the "source of law and the standard [shaping] Muslim ethics and values" (Mernissi, 1991, p. 1). They were as such making a close textual analysis, a central strategy in their work on text as the written, the Qur'an, and the spoken, the Hadīth.

DECONSTRUCTING THE *HIJABS*

The first step in *deveiling* the *hijab* discourse and how it came into being as a gendering discourse is to deconstruct the *hijabs* in the canonical Arabic dictionary, *Lisan Al 'Arab*, and the most fundamental and sacred Islamic text, the Qur'an. For this purpose, I draw on the exhaustive research of Fatima Mernissi (1991) and Lynda Clarke (2003), *ijtihad*, a major strategy of Islamic rigorous research and their use of the tools of a major classical Islamic methodology of exegesis, *tafsir*. Particularly, I draw on Mernissi's and Clarke's deconstructive textual analysis of the *hijabs'* linguistic scope in Arabic and the *hijabs'* decontextualized popular interpretations in the relevant Qura'nic verses. This is feminist *ijtihad* (Mashhour, 2005) or what others also call gender *ijtihad*, an engagement in gender struggle through acts of "(re)thinking" or "intellectual struggle to understand" (Badran, 2008, p. 311).[1]

Additionally, in this *deveiling* process, I highlight Mernissi and Clarke's exposure of "the nature of the knowledge and knowledge building" (Hesse-Biber, 2007, p. 84), and the "regimes of truth" that occupied the dominant space creating certain unquestionable "truths" about *muslim* females on the basis of their gender "difference." Besides the textual analysis, the exposure of the positionalities of androcentric Muslim scholars who controlled language and controlled access to interpretations of the text, hegemonized the *hijabs'* fixed meaning, and thus, socially constructed a gendering discourse inscribed on *muslimat's* bodies for centuries.

The *Hijabs'* Reduced Linguistic Scope in Arabic

The first step to deconstruct the *hijabs* is to expose their reduced linguistic scope in the canonical dictionary of *Lisan Al 'Arab*. By using a literary or philological methodology of exegesis (Barazangi, 2004), one classical Islamic interpretive tool, Mernissi argued that *Lisan Al 'Arab* of Ibn Manzur (630–712 A.H.[2]) a major Arabic dictionary and a canonical source of meaning reflecting the dominant usage of words in arab-*muslim* societies—had played a major role in reducing the *hijab's* linguistic scope or hiding its four visible and invisible dimensions. Given that in Arabic, the noun *hijab* (veil) is based on the root verb *hjb* which means to cover, hide, shelter, protect, and establish a boundary, barrier, border, screen, curtain, or threshold (*Lisan Al 'Arab*), Mernissi (1991) asserted that the *hijab* is four-dimensional, and that they "often blend into one another" (p. 93). That is,

> The first dimension [of the *hijab*] is a visual, one: to hide something from sight.... The second dimension is spatial, to separate, to mark a border, to establish a threshold.... And finally, the third dimension is ethical: it belongs to the realm of the forbidden. (Mernissi, 1991, p. 93)

Lisan Al 'Arab defined the *hijab*, (1) as *sitr*, literally a curtain, and, (2) as *hijabah*, the cover of the sacred shrine of *Ka'ba* in Mecca[3] and the curtain separating the caliph from the members of his court (Mernissi, 1991). In these exclusive definitions, this widely used and authoritative

Arabic dictionary not only limited the *hijab* to its spatial and hypervisual dimensions but also as such disregarded its third ethical dimension. As such, the *hijab*'s physical—visual and spatial—became easily fixed and were rendered more popular. That is, the simplified and reduced visual and spatial meaning of the *hijab* in *Lisan Al 'Arab* became widely circulated obscuring its other nonvisual and subtler meanings especially those that could help more *muslims* make sense of their complex lives in all contexts.

More important, Mernissi highlighted that *Lisan Al 'Arab* also eliminated a fourth spiritual dimension of the *hijab*, which many Muslims, devote their lives to and aspire to uncover or cross in order to approach the knowledge of Allah. It is the *hijab* that *muslims* should pursue to cross because "a person has access to boundless spiritual horizons, which the Muslim must aspire to ... [and this] *hijab* is a negative phenomenon, a disturbance, a disability [that makes a Muslim] not perceive the divine light in [her/] his soul" (Mernissi, 1991, p. 95). This *hijab* is prominent in the Qur'an and it is referred to as a "spiritual" separation from knowledge. It is the *hijab* that *muslims* are called to pay more attention to, reflect on, and cross in pursuit of knowing Allah more deeply. For example, the following Qur'anic verse, in which Allah warned *muslims* to elude the *hijab* that prevents them from knowing Allah and the Prophet's message or Islam's message,

⁴ وَقَالُوا قُلُوبُنَا فِي أَكِنَّةٍ مِّمَّا تَدْعُونَا إِلَيْهِ وَفِي آذَانِنَا وَقْرٌ وَمِن بَيْنِنَا وَبَيْنِكَ حِجَابٌ فَاعْمَلْ إِنَّنَا عَامِلُونَ. (القرآن الكريم، ٤١:٥)

And they say: Our hearts are protected from that unto which thou (O Muhammad) callest us, and in our ears there is a deafness, and between us and thee there is a veil [*hijab*]. Act, then. Lo! we also shall be acting. (The Qur'an, 41:5)⁵

In committing to uncover and cross this spiritual *hijab*, a Muslim takes on a sacred pursuit to move beyond or reverse the earthly or physical *hijabs* that block one's "extraordinary capacities for multiple perceptions" (Mernissi, 1991, p. 95). As such, Mernissi clarified that the fourth *hijab* is essentially a "negative phenomenon" that imprisons or veils off a Muslim's consciousness and keeps her/him away from knowledge and knowing (Mernissi, 1991). With this, Mernissi argued that the spiritual *hijab* is displaced or erased and it is forcefully masked by the visual and spatial *hijabs* especially in relation to women.

Mernissi (1991) illustrated in this philological analysis that the *hijab* is not a one-dimensional term or it is not only a scrap of cloth that inscribed the bodies of *muslimat* for centuries. The *hijab* is more than a dress for women and not only a curtain that separates women from men. Rather, the *hijab* is multidimensional that may open many possibilities in relearning and reusing its other invisible, ethical, and spiritual, meanings. That is, expanding the meaning of the *hijab* from the visible to the invisible and subtle, from two commonly circulated representations to four, I argue that the *hijab* is a notion of multiple and shifting meanings. In its multiplicity and fluidity, the *hijab* has the potential to open new horizons for *muslims* searching for deeper knowledge and seeking understanding of their own complex lived experiences of *muslimness*. Thus, *deveiling* the *hijabs* linguistically is a process and a tool to counter the hegemony of the gendering discourse. It is also the frame and focus of this book.

With this deconstructive philological analysis and utilizing language as a constitutive force, Mernissi worked with the "inconsistencies and weaknesses of meaning that are inherent in the text" (Gannon & Davies, 2007, p. 85) to deveil or reinterpret the decontextualized *hijab* Qur'anic verses as I illustrate in the following section.

The *Hijabs'* (De)Contextualized Interpretations in Qur'anic Verses

The second step to deconstruct the *hijabs* is to expose their four visible and invisible dimensions in the popular decontextualized interpretations of all the relevant *hijab* Qur'anic *ayyat*—verses. The Qur'an, Islam's fundamental and most sacred text (Kugle, 2010), is a text of revelations or a collection of "the divine words inspired by God in the Prophet" (Mernissi, 1991, p. 217). For too long the interpretations of Qur'anic verses, and thus, the resulting rulings that became taken-for-granted "Islamic" norms, including the "conception of the meaning of gender and the arrangements regarding women" (Ahmed, 1992, p. 239) were exclusive to the dominant classes of male scholars (Clarke, 2003; Mernissi, 1991; Wadud, 1999). According to Leila Ahmed (1992),

> From the start, the interpretation of the meaning of gender in the dominant society ... [were] contested. Establishment Islam's version of the Islamic message survived as the sole legitimate interpretation not because it was the only possible interpretation but because it was the interpretation of the politically dominant [male elite (Mernissi, 1991)]—those who had the power to outlaw and eradicate other readings as "heretical."... Just as with the other monotheistic (and indeed nonmonotheistic) religions, what the import of Islam was and what its significance for human societies and that again today are open to a range of interpretations, including feminist interpretations. (p. 239)

However, in the past 30 years, Mernissi like many *arab-muslim* feminists and Islamic feminists (Ahmed, 1992; Badran, 2009; Barazangi, 2004,

2009; El Saadawi, 1998; Mernissi, 1991; Wadud, 1999) accessed the sacred text directly and began to challenge the unquestionable androcentric interpretations of gender and the implications of their resulting rulings. More currently, other scholars in the disciplines of sociology, ethics, and Islamic studies began challenging the heteronormative interpretations of sexuality in the Qur'an and the Hadīth (Ali, 2006; Kugle, 2010). This is even a more daring project but it is drawing on and intersecting with the previous feminist efforts of reinterpreting gender in Islam (Ahmed, 1992; Mernissi, 1991).

In the following step of deconstructing the *hijabs*, doing a textual analysis and contextualizing all the relevant *hijab* Qur'anic *ayyat*, Clarke (2003) and Mernissi (1991) utilized the major classical methodology of Islamic exegesis (*tafsir*) and analogical reasoning (*qiyas*). Traditionally, these methods produced the *fiqh* (deep understandings) or the "major collection of the jurisprudential interpretations of the Qur'an and jurisprudential rulings based on the Hadīth. The *fiqh* outcomes became mistakenly known as *the* sacred Islamic Jurisprudence or Sharia,[6] "religious legal corpus" (Badran, 2009, p. 217), and thus, were unquestionable. Importantly, the *fiqh* was compiled during the formative years of Islam and at the beginning of the ʿAbbasid Caliphate (started A.D. 750 or 132 H.A.) (Ahmed, 1992). Badran explains,

> Islamic jurisprudence (*fiqh*), consolidated in its classical form in the ninth century, was itself heavily saturated with the patriarchal thinking and behaviors of the day. It is this patriarchally-inflected jurisprudence that has informed the various contemporary formulations of the shari'a. (2009, p. 247)

However, the canon of *fiqh* had been fixed or made the gates to *ijtihad* inaccessible by the tenth century CE (Badran, 2009). According to Ahmed (1992), jurisprudential rulings often represented the dominance of the political vision of the Abbasid dynasty. On the "problem" of interpretation of the Qur'an as Sharia, or the legal opinion constructed as final, unquestionable, and sacred, Ahmed (1992) asserted that,

> the Quranic precepts consists mainly of broad, general propositions chiefly of an ethical nature, rather than specific legalistic formulations. As scholars have pointed out, the Quran raises many problems [when and if considered] as a legislative document; it by no means provides a simple and straightforward code of law. On the contrary, the specific content of the laws derivable from the Quran depended greatly on the interpretations that legists chose to bring to it and the elements of its complex utterances that they chose to give weight to. (p. 88)

More importantly, since these collections of *fiqh* are secondary to the Qur'an and the Hadīth (Barazangi, 2009), Mernissi and Clarke, like many other *muslim* scholars throughout the centuries after Mohammed's death, did their own *ijtihad*, rigorous research, by turning directly to the Qur'an and the Hadīth. They challenged the epistemologies and positionalities of those who produced the knowledge or the *fiqh*, and consequently produced and enforced Sharia. They challenged mainly those canonical interpretations and practices that were dismissive of gender justice. As such, they also challenged the dominant political rulers of the time that legitimized their power through the unquestionable *fiqh*. They delegitimized the interpretation of the dominant male elite of scholars (Mernissi, 19991) and the very institutions that perpetuated patriarchy (Ahmed, 1992). Similar to other "Western" critical feminists who challenged for example science the past few decades, these *arab-muslim* feminists have argued that, the Islamic *fiqh* is a knowledge production paradigm that is historically rooted in another kind of positivist epistemology subscribing to the tenets of verification, generalization, objectivity, value-neutrality (Hesse-Biber & Piatelli, 2007). In this case, the male elite of *fiqh* scholars rooted their interpretations in the generalizability and objectivity of the unquestionable sacredness of the Qur'an that is "completely independent of historical and sociological influences" (Ahmed, 1992, p. 90). Many *muslim* groups, such as the Sufis and Qarmatians, throughout the centuries, have challenged the monopoly of the truth and the elite scholars' declaration of its "version on Islam to be absolute" (Ahmed, 1992, p. 94). Like these groups who have presented radical interpretations of the Qur'an emphasizing its inner and spiritual meanings, *arab-muslim* feminists of this time are beginning to challenge the prevailing "letter-bound approach of orthodoxy" (Ahmed, 1992, p. 96) in the interpretations of the Qur'an in relation to gender justice and equity. Thus, in their work, these *arab-muslim* feminists have challenged Islamic androcentric exegesis that has produced for centuries the *fiqh* that supported and maintained a hierarchical approach to knowledge building. This approach was not only closed to reinterpretation but also more significantly closed to women scholars (Ahmed, 1992; Badran, 2009; Barazangi, 2004, 2009; El Saadawi, 1998; Mernissi, 1991; Wadud, 1999).

To embark on this task of reinterpreting the sacred text, several *arab-muslim* feminists expanded the use of *asbab al nuzul* (reasons of revelations), the same tool of classical Islamic exegesis that produced the androcentric textual interpretation of the *hijabs'* Qur'anic verses. They expanded its classical use from uncovering the "occasion upon which, (or, sometimes, because of which)" (Wadud, 1999, p. 30) a certain Qur'anic verse was revealed to uncovering the larger "context of the revelation" (Barazangi, 2004, p. 29). That is, they used *asbab al nuzul* as a contextualizing and historicizing tool of reinterpreting the sacred text. Moreover, since these Qur'anic verses or revelations were "intended to resolve real-life problems that the Prophet confronted or questions that the new converts asked him" (Mernissi, 1991, p. 217), *asbab al nuzul*, is an essential tool for making the Qur'anic verse easily comprehendible, and thus, accessible and applicable to the daily experiences of all *muslims* in any context.

To expand on Clarke's (2003) and Mernissi's (1991) work of deconstructing the *hijabs'* four visible and invisible dimensions in the popular decontextualized interpretations of all the relevant *hijab* Qur'anic verses, I took two steps of *deveiling*. First, I have searched for all the *hijab* and other veiling terms in Qur'anic verses (16 verses—as listed below). These included, (1) the derivatives of the verb *hjb*—*hijab* and *mahjoob*, (2) other veil terms—*akkinnah, ghishyyah, ghita'* and *dhulumat*, and (3) clothing and modesty terms—*jalābībihinna* and *khumrīhinna*. Accordingly, I presented a textual analysis of all the verses with these terms and divided them in relation to, (1) spatial *hijabs* and privacy (2 verses), (2) the spiritual *hijabs* and the pursuit of deeper knowledge (10 verses), (3) the visual *hijabs* and modest clothing of all Muslims (2 verses), and (4) the ethical *hijabs* and the respect of the Prophet's wives (2 verses). Second, I highlighted and discussed Mernissi's contextualization of these verses that have become the most popular misused and misinterpreted, and thus, hegemonizing *hijab* Qur'anic verses.

Two Verses on Spatial *Hijabs* and Privacy

The *hijab* as a noun, the object that veils a space, appears in only two Qur'anic verses (19:17; 33:53). In these two verses, the term *hijab* appears in its spatial dimension and when contextualized it does not mean the separation between men and women. In the first verse (33:53), the *hijab* refers to the door curtain that specifically protected the privacy of The Prophet on one of his wedding nights. In the second verse (19:17), the *hijab* refers to an abstract screen or a secluded place that protected the privacy of Maryam giving birth to prophet Issa, Jesus.

First, the *hijab* appears in the most infamous Qur'anic verse,

يَا أَيُّهَا الَّذِينَ آمَنُوا لَا تَدْخُلُوا بُيُوتَ النَّبِيِّ إِلَّا أَن يُؤْذَنَ لَكُمْ إِلَى طَعَامٍ غَيْرَ نَاظِرِينَ إِنَاهُ وَلَكِنْ إِذَا دُعِيتُمْ فَادْخُلُوا فَإِذَا طَعِمْتُمْ

فَانتَشِرُوا وَلَا مُسْتَأْنِسِينَ لِحَدِيثٍ إِنَّ ذَلِكُمْ كَانَ يُؤْذِي النَّبِيَّ فَيَسْتَحْيِي مِنكُمْ وَاللَّهُ لَا يَسْتَحْيِي مِنَ الْحَقِّ وَإِذَا سَأَلْتُمُوهُنَّ مَتَاعًا

فَاسْأَلُوهُنَّ مِن وَرَاءِ حِجَابٍ ذَلِكُمْ أَطْهَرُ لِقُلُوبِكُمْ وَقُلُوبِهِنَّ وَمَا كَانَ لَكُمْ أَن تُؤْذُوا رَسُولَ اللَّهِ وَلَا أَن تَنكِحُوا أَزْوَاجَهُ مِن بَعْدِهِ أَبَدًا

إِنَّ ذَلِكُمْ كَانَ عِندَ اللَّهِ عَظِيمًا. (القرآن الكريم ، ٣٣:٥٣)

O ye who believe! Enter not the Prophet's houses, until leave is given you -
for a meal, (and then) not (so early as) to wait for its preparation: but when
ye are invited, enter; and when ye have taken your meal, disperse, without
seeking familiar talk. Such (behavior) annoys the Prophet: he is ashamed to
dismiss you, but Allah is not ashamed (to tell you) the Truth. And when ye
ask (his ladies) for anything ye want ask them from before a screen [*hijab*]:
that makes for greater purity for your hearts and for theirs. Nor is it right
for you that ye should annoy Allah's Messenger, or that ye should marry his
widows after him at any time. Truly, such a thing is in Allah's sight an enor-
mity. (The Qur'an, 33:53)

This verse was revealed to the Prophet on His wedding night to his
cousin Zaynab bint Jahsh. It signified the "descent of the *hijab*" (Mernissi,
1991, p. 85) explaining two simultaneous events taking place in different
realms. Mernissi (1991) contextualized this verse and explained,

On the other hand, God's revelation to the Prophet, which is in the intellectual realm; and on the other hand the descent of a cloth *hijab*, a material
object, a curtain that the Prophet draws between himself and the man who
was at the entrance of nuptial chamber. (p. 85)

In this, Mernissi brought to light how this very popular verse (33:53)
interpreted out of context, has institutionalized the *hijab* in Muslim
women's lives and constituted their separation from the public sphere.
Citing the account of the Prophet's wedding night to his cousin Zaynab
bint Jahsh (Sahih Al Bukhari, *hadīth* 5166),[7] and the interpretation of a
credible Muslim scholar, Al Tabari, Mernissi asserted that the *hijab* is a
border between two specific men and not men and women (Mernissi,
1991). It is literally a curtain or screen that "'descended' in the bedroom
of the wedded pair to protect their intimacy and exclude a third person—
in this case, Anas Ibn Malik, one of the Prophet's Companions" (p. 85)—
boy helper who accompanies him almost everywhere. The *hijab* came
down to exclude one man from being intrusive on the Prophets home and
His bridal chamber. This verse was calling for this one male guest to consider the spatial separation in the Prophet's private dwelling at a specific
incident, his wedding night. It was requesting him to respect the
Prophet's right to intimacy with His bride, and thus, right to privacy in
His own house (Clarke, 2003; Mernissi, 1991). In other words, this verse
referred to the specific incident in which "the Prophet had just got married and was impatient to be alone with his new wife ... was not able to get
rid of the small group of tactless guests who remained lost in conversation" for too long after the invitees left (Mernissi, 1991, p. 86).

Similarly important, by historicizing this verse, Mernissi further
exposed that it was revealed to the Prophet at the beginning of fifth year

of the Hijrah (A.D. 627), a year of stagnation following a defeat in Uhud battle (3 A.H.). This was a turbulent military time for the new Muslims at the beginning of the journey of Islam still living in exile in Al Medina. That is, this was a time when the Prophet most needed the peace of mind, and thus, Allah's request in this verse was directed at the Companions to observe social tact or "niceties that seemed to lack, like entering dwelling without asking permission" (Mernissi, 1991, p. 92).

Mernissi's (1991) contextualized and historicized interpretation made it clear that the *hijab* in this verse did not mean, "to put the barrier between a man and a woman, but between two men" (Mernissi, 1991, p. 85). Mernissi asserted that,

> it comes to saying that the Prophet, during a troubled period at the beginning of Islam, pronounced a verse that was so exceptional and determining for the Muslim religion that it introduced a breach in space that can be understood to be a separation of the public from the private, or indeed the profane from the sacred, but which was to turn into a segregation of the sexes. (Mernissi, 1991, p. 101)

That is, it did not mean to separate or protect the wives of the Prophet nor all of Muslim women from all men. It did not mean to exclude all Muslim women from public life and "split the Muslim space" (p. 92). Even if we were to generalize the meaning of the *hijab* in this verse to more than separating male guests in this particular wedding night from the bridal room of the Prophet, it would refer to a call for all Muslims to respect the privacy of others (Mernissi, 1991). Thus, this verse referred to the spatial *hijab* only as the border between the private and public spaces specifically in relation to the Prophet's life at the time (5 A.H.).

Second, the term *hijab* appears one more time in its spatial dimensions in the Qur'anic verse,

فَٱتَّخَذَتْ مِن دُونِهِمْ حِجَابًا فَأَرْسَلْنَا إِلَيْهَا رُوحَنَا فَتَمَثَّلَ لَهَا بَشَرًا سَوِيًّا. (القرآن الكريم، ١٩:١٧)

She placed a screen [*hijab*] from them; then We sent to her Our Ruh [angel Jibril (Gabriel)], and he appeared before her in the form of a man in all respects. (The Qur'an, 19:17)

Again, by exposing or quoting the full verse, this *hijab* referred to a secluded space that acted as an abstract veil separating Maryam in a specific incident. The screen in this verse was meant to separate Maryam from outsiders while giving birth to prophet Issa, a holy incident. Again, this *hijab* verse was not about the spatial physical border between men and women or between women and public life. It specifically represented the spiritual protection of Maryam giving birth to prophet Issa.

Ten Verses on the Spiritual *Hijabs* and the Knowing of Allah or the Pursuit of Deeper Knowledge

The term *hijab* (noun), the object that is used to veil, and the term *mah-joob* (adjective), the person who is being veiled, appear in six Qur'anic verses (7:46; 17:45; 38:32; 41:5; 42:51, and 83:15). Other veil terms appear, *akkinnah, ghishyyah, ghita', and dhulumat*, appear in four Qur'anic verses (6:25; 12:107; 18:57; and 50:22). In these 10 verses, the terms *hijab, mahjoob, akkinnah, ghishyyah, ghita', and dhulumat* do not refer at all to the visible and physical *hijab*, or to the spatial separation between men and women whether visually or spatially (Mernissi, 1991). That is, in 10 (out of 16) *hijab*-related Qur'anic verses the *hijab* appears in its spiritual dimension, as the cover or barrier that prevents and excludes the believers from "the privileges and spiritual grace" (Mernissi, 1991, p. 97) of knowing Allah and the Prophet's message. In other words, the *hijab* in these Qur'anic verses does not represent the separator between men and women but on the contrary, it calls for the pursuit of deeper knowledge.

According to Al-Tarbari, Mernissi asserted that the *hijab* and *mahjoob* in the following two Qur'anic verses (41:5 and 83:15), expressed difficulties that Quraysh, a tribe in Mecca, traditionally polytheistic, had in understanding the monotheistic message of Muhammad (1991, p. 97).

وَقَالُوا قُلُوبُنَا فِي أَكِنَّةٍ مِّمَّا تَدْعُونَا إِلَيْهِ وَفِي آذَانِنَا وَقْرٌ وَمِن بَيْنِنَا وَبَيْنِكَ حِجَابٌ فَاعْمَلْ إِنَّنَا عَامِلُونَ. (القرآن الكريم، ٤١:٥)

And they say: Our hearts are protected from that unto which thou (O Muhammad) callest us, and in our ears there is a deafness, and between us and thee there is a veil [*hijab*]. Act, then. Lo! we also shall be acting. (The Qur'an, 41:5)

كَلَّا إِنَّهُمْ عَن رَّبِّهِمْ يَوْمَئِذٍ لَّمَحْجُوبُونَ. (القرآن الكريم، ٨٣:١٥)

Nay! Surely they (evil-doers) will be veiled [mhajuboon] from seeing their Lord that Day. (The Qur'an, 83:15)

The *hijab* in the above verses signified a difference or conflict in religion between the believers of Islam and those who are "evil-doers." Those who are most blinded and punished by a *hijab* are the nonbelievers, the polytheists (Mernissi, 1991). Thus, the *hijab* has a negative meaning on all nonbelievers or those Muslims, women and men, who do not pursue spiritual grace. Mernissi asserted that,

> it is strange indeed to observe the modern course of this concept, which from the beginning had such a strongly negative connotation in the Koran. The very sign of the person who is damned, excluded from the privileges of spiritual grace to which the Muslim has access, is claimed in our day as a symbol of Muslim identity, manna [divine and spiritual nourishment] for the Muslim woman. (1991, p. 97)

Moreover, other veil terms—*akkinnah, ghishyyah, ghita', and dhulumat*—appeared in four more Qur'anic verses (6:25; 12:107; 18:57; and 50:22) and they were not referring to women at all nor did they call for covering their bodies. These verses emphasized the significance of the spiritual *hijab*. They were a call for all Muslims to cross the spiritual *hijab* in pursuit of knowing Allah and the Prophet's message.

وَمِنْهُم مَّن يَسْتَمِعُ إِلَيْكَ وَجَعَلْنَا عَلَى قُلُوبِهِمْ أَكِنَّةً أَن يَفْقَهُوهُ وَفِي آذَانِهِمْ وَقْرًا وَإِن يَرَوْا كُلَّ آيَةٍ لاَّ يُؤْمِنُواْ بِهَا حَتَّى إِذَا جَاؤُوكَ يُجَادِلُونَكَ يَقُولُ الَّذِينَ كَفَرُواْ إِنْ هَذَا إِلاَّ أَسَاطِيرُ الأَوَّلِينَ. (القرآن الكريم، ٦:٢٥)

Of them there are some who (pretend to) listen to thee; but We have thrown veils [akkinnah] on their hearts, So they understand it not, and deafness in their ears; if they saw every one of the signs, not they will believe in them; in so much that when they come to thee, they (but) dispute with thee; the Unbelievers say: These are nothing but tales of the ancients. (The Qur'an, 6:25)

أَفَأَمِنُواْ أَن تَأْتِيَهُمْ غَاشِيَةٌ مِّنْ عَذَابِ اللّهِ أَوْ تَأْتِيَهُمُ السَّاعَةُ بَغْتَةً وَهُمْ لاَ يَشْعُرُونَ. (القرآن الكريم، ١٢:١٠٧)

Do they then feel secure from the coming against them of the covering veil [ghishayyah] of the wrath of Allah, or of the coming against them of the (final) Hour all of a sudden while they perceive not? (The Qur'an, 12:107)

وَمَنْ أَظْلَمُ مِمَّن ذُكِّرَ بِآيَاتِ رَبِّهِ فَأَعْرَضَ عَنْهَا وَنَسِيَ مَا قَدَّمَتْ يَدَاهُ إِنَّا جَعَلْنَا عَلَى قُلُوبِهِمْ أَكِنَّةً أَن يَفْقَهُوهُ وَفِي آذَانِهِمْ وَقْرًا وَإِن تَدْعُهُمْ إِلَى الْهُدَى فَلَن يَهْتَدُوا إِذًا أَبَدًا. (القرآن الكريم، ١٨:٥٧)

And who doth more wrong than one who is reminded of the Signs of his Lord, but turns away from them, forgetting the (deeds) which his hands have sent forth? Verily We have set veils [akkinnah] over their hearts lest they should understand this, and over their ears, deafness, if thou callest them to guidance, even then will they never accept guidance. (The Qur'an, 18:57)

لَقَدْ كُنتَ فِي غَفْلَةٍ مِّنْ هَذَا فَكَشَفْنَا عَنكَ غِطَاءَكَ فَبَصَرُكَ الْيَوْمَ حَدِيدٌ. (القرآن الكريم، ٢٢:٥٠)

(It will be said:) "Thou wast heedless of this; now have We removed thy veil, and sharp is thy sight this Day!" (The Qur'an, 50:22)

Without contextualization, intensive reflection, and rigor in studying the text, the spiritual dimension of the *hijab* would stay underemphasized, and thus, *muslims*' vision of Allah's truth would be obscured. Even when the spiritual *hijab* is referenced in this many Qur'anic verses, a major priority in the message of Islam, approaching piety through the pursuit of deeper knowledge was obstructed.

Two Verses on the Visual *Hijabs* and Modesty of All Muslims

In reference to women's clothing, the terms *jalābībihinna* and *khumrīhinna* appear in two more verses (33:59 and 24:31). In these two verses, the term *hijab* appears in its visual dimension. When verse (33:59) is contextualized, the term *jalābībihinna* (their cloaks) does not mean the separation between men and women or the obsession over covering the bodies of *muslim* women. And when verse (24:31) is read in combination with verse (24:30), modesty is instructed on both Muslim men and women. Ahmed emphasized that these two Qur'anic verses are the only verses that refer to women's clothing. She wrote,

It is nowhere explicitly prescribed in the Quran; the only verses dealing with women's clothing, aside from those already quoted, instruct women to guard their private parts and throw a scarf over their bosoms. (1992, p. 55)

The first verse (33:59) about dressing cloaks, *jalābīb*, is the second most renowned so-called *hijab* Qur'anic verse after verse 33:53 and the verse that institutionalized Muslim women's dress (Ahmed, 1992; Mernissi, 1991). In this verse, the *hijab*-related term *jalābīhinna* refers to the cloaks of the Prophets' wives, the protector of their safety, in a specific context. It reads,

يَا أَيُّهَا النَّبِيُّ قُل لِّأَزْوَاجِكَ وَبَنَاتِكَ وَنِسَاء الْمُؤْمِنِينَ يُدْنِينَ عَلَيْهِنَّ مِن جَلَابِيبِهِنَّ ذَلِكَ أَدْنَى أَن يُعْرَفْنَ فَلَا يُؤْذَيْنَ وَكَانَ اللَّهُ غَفُورًا رَّحِيمًا. (القرآن الكريم، ٣٣:٥٩)

O Prophet! say to your wives and your daughters and the women of the believers that to draw [a part] of their cloaks [jalābīhinna] close around them; that is more suitable, so that they will not be recognised and annoyed; and Allah is Forgiving, Merciful. (The Qur'an, 33:59)

At the time (A.D. 622 to A.D. 630) in Al Medina a problem surfaced when women had to go out in the open to defecate or even walk anywhere in the streets (Mernissi, 1991). Highlighting this context, Mernissi and others explained that at this time Muslims did not have private "out houses" for one and when they walked in the streets they ran into "immoral persons who, if they were not wearing veils ... would try to accost them" (Clarke, 2003, p. 275). In other words, women, whatever their status, were being harassed in the streets of Al Medina. Once *muslim* women of that time reported this problem to the Prophet, he sent his representatives to question those men who misbehaved. They explained "their behavior by saying: 'We only practice *ta'arrud* with women we believe to be slaves'—thus excusing themselves by claiming confusion about the identity of the women they approached" (Mernissi, 1991, p. 180).

According to Mernissi's contextualized reinterpretation, this verse (33:59) was revealed to the Prophet to deter the violence against women prevalent in the streets of Al Medina. This problematic practice of *ta'arrud*—harassment—and *zina*—forbidden adultery became the very focus against which the message of Islam was struggling at the time (Mernissi, 1991). The Prophet wanted to mainly assure the safety of His wives and other Muslim women—the so-called free women—and thus, protect them from male harassers.

In the unsafe streets of Al Medina, this verse instructed the Prophet's wives and Muslim women generally "to draw their cloaks around them so that they could be recognized as believers and thus not be molested" (Ahmed, 1992, p. 54). That is, the cloak drawn around the Prophet's wives and Muslim women's bodies was meant to protect them from the male harassers by differentiating them from the women who were slaves at the time and were still reduced to prostitution. This verse was revealed to the Prophet at a time when his Companion 'Umar ibn al Khatab was urging the Prophet to "seclude his wives, though unsuccessfully ... and to guard [them] against the insults of the 'hypocrites' ... who would abuse Muhammad's wives and then claim that they had taken them as slaves" (Ahmed 1992, p. 54).

Sadly, this verse in its call for protecting only Muslim women with a piece of cloth in a certain circumstance not only deemphasized the male's responsibility in the violence against women in the street of Al Medina but it also was a marker between the believing women and female salves of the time. In other words, males' violence and disrespect towards women of another religion and class was acceptable and Muslim women were targeted as the problem to be hidden and protected (Mernissi, 1991). Under the circumstances the Muslims were living in at the time in Al Medina and the "unambiguously patriarchal society" (Ahmed, 1992, p. 55), this verse (33:59) along with verse (33:53) Ahmed asserted that the seclusion and the cover of Muslim women's bodies became institutionalized.

By disregarding the context of revelation in which men were still constructing women as objects of sexual desire as they have been before Islam, this verse has become the reference for disciplining Muslim women's dress, movement, and participation in public life all together (Mernissi, 1991). In other words, this verse was meant to resolve the issue of respecting women in public and stopping male's violent sexual behavior against them—whether they were free or salves. It was *not* meant to insist on and emphasize the taken-for-granted commonly used justification of this verse that the "danger is posed *by* [added emphasis] women as the prime reason for *hijab*" (Clarke, 2003, p. 275), that is, the covering of women's bodies.

Importantly, the above verse did not introduce a new clothing item to cover Muslim women bodies in public. They were already wearing cloaks as protectors from the heat of the desert (Mernissi, 1991) and "in accord with a long-standing Semitic custom" (Clarke, 2003, p. 233). Ahmed added,

> Veiling was apparently not introduced into Arabia by Muhammad but already existed among some classes, particularly in the towns, though it was probably more prevalent in the countries that the Arabs has contact with, such as Syria and Palestine. In those areas, as in Arab, it was connected with social status, as was it use among Greeks, Romans, Jews, and Assyrians, all of whom practiced veiling to some degree. (1992, p. 55)

The second most reiterated *hijab*-related verse (24:31) that helped institutionalize Muslim women's dress, actually instructs Muslim women to be modest. In Arabic, modesty or *al hishma* means staying away from what is embarrassing and angering (*Lisan Al ʿArab*). Given that modesty represents the act by which a Muslim maintains her/his moderation, humility, and respect or shying away from the forbiddens, the popular use and interpretation of this verse focuses on women's modesty only and mainly her dress (*khumrīhinna*). As such, modesty of Muslims is reduced as the taken-for-granted order of covering only Muslim women's bodies in public and in the presence of men who are not from their immediate family. In other words, the other aspects of modesty in behavior and attitude required of all Muslims are deemphasized. This verse reads,

وَقُل لِّلْمُؤْمِنَاتِ يَغْضُضْنَ مِنْ أَبْصَارِهِنَّ وَيَحْفَظْنَ فُرُوجَهُنَّ وَلَا يُبْدِينَ زِينَتَهُنَّ إِلَّا مَا ظَهَرَ مِنْهَا وَلْيَضْرِبْنَ بِخُمُرِهِنَّ عَلَى جُيُوبِهِنَّ وَلَا
يُبْدِينَ زِينَتَهُنَّ إِلَّا لِبُعُولَتِهِنَّ أَوْ آبَائِهِنَّ أَوْ آبَاءِ بُعُولَتِهِنَّ أَوْ أَبْنَائِهِنَّ أَوْ أَبْنَاءِ بُعُولَتِهِنَّ أَوْ إِخْوَانِهِنَّ أَوْ بَنِي إِخْوَانِهِنَّ أَوْ
نِسَائِهِنَّ أَوْ مَا مَلَكَتْ أَيْمَانُهُنَّ أَوِ التَّابِعِينَ غَيْرِ أُولِي الْإِرْبَةِ مِنَ الرِّجَالِ أَوِ الطِّفْلِ الَّذِينَ لَمْ يَظْهَرُوا عَلَى عَوْرَاتِ النِّسَاءِ وَلَا يَضْرِبْنَ
بِأَرْجُلِهِنَّ لِيُعْلَمَ مَا يُخْفِينَ مِن زِينَتِهِنَّ وَتُوبُوا إِلَى اللَّهِ جَمِيعًا أَيُّهَا الْمُؤْمِنُونَ لَعَلَّكُمْ تُفْلِحُونَ. (القرآن الكريم، ٢٤:٣١)

And say to the believing women that they cast down their looks and guard their private parts and do not display their ornaments except what appears thereof, and let them wear their head-coverings [*khumrīhinna*] over their bosoms, and not display their ornaments except to their husbands or their fathers, or the fathers of their husbands, or their sons, or the sons of their husbands, or their brothers, or their brothers' sons, or their sisters' sons, or their women, or those whom their right hands possess, or the male servants not having need (of women), or the children who have not attained knowledge of what is hidden of women; and let them not strike their feet so that what they hide of their ornaments may be known; and turn to Allah all of you, O believers! so that you may be successful. (The Qur'an, 24:31)

Mernissi (1991) argued that this verse is usually cited by conveniently dismissing its chronology in the chapter. That is, the preceding verse (24:30) in which Allah also asked male Muslim believers to act and dress modestly is disregarded. This verse reads,

قُل لِّلْمُؤْمِنِينَ يَغُضُّوا مِنْ أَبْصَارِهِمْ وَيَحْفَظُوا فُرُوجَهُمْ ذَلِكَ أَزْكَى لَهُمْ إِنَّ اللَّهَ خَبِيرٌ بِمَا يَصْنَعُونَ.(القرآن الكريم، ٢٤:٣٠)

Tell the believing men to lower their gaze and be modest. That is purer for them. Lo! Allah is aware of what they do. (The Qur'an, 24:30)

Additionally, this "deliberate" dismissal of Muslim males responsibility towards modesty which is more consistent with andocentric interpretation of the *hijab* supports Mernissi's argument about the tendency of later exegesis scholars to "reify the material [they] seek to explain" (Clarke, 2003, p. 227). That is, the limitation of the *hijab*'s meaning to its nonspiritual or only to its visual and spatial dimensions is what normalizes the body of a woman as the problem or the object to protect.

Two Verses on the Ethical *Hijabs* and the Respect of the Prophet's Wives

The final two *hijab*-related Qur'anic verses (33:32 and 33:33), call mainly the Prophet's wives to observe the ethical *hijab*. Again, these two verses have been inaccurately cited to support the seclusion of Muslim women in the private realm. They read,

يَا نِسَاء النَّبِيِّ لَسْتُنَّ كَأَحَدٍ مِّنَ النِّسَاء إِنِ اتَّقَيْتُنَّ فَلَا تَخْضَعْنَ بِالْقَوْلِ فَيَطْمَعَ الَّذِي فِي قَلْبِهِ مَرَضٌ وَقُلْنَ قَوْلًا مَّعْرُوفًا.(القرآن الكريم،

(٣٢:٣٣

O wives of the Prophet! you are not like any other of the women, if you will be on your guard, then be not soft in (your) speech, lest he in whose heart is a disease yearn, and speak a good word. (The Qur'an, 33:32)

وَقَرْنَ فِي بُيُوتِكُنَّ وَلَا تَبَرَّجْنَ تَبَرُّجَ الْجَاهِلِيَّةِ الْأُولَى وَأَقِمْنَ الصَّلَاةَ وَآتِينَ الزَّكَاةَ وَأَطِعْنَ اللَّهَ وَرَسُولَهُ إِنَّمَا يُرِيدُ اللَّهُ لِيُذْهِبَ عَنكُمُ الرِّجْسَ أَهْلَ الْبَيْتِ وَيُطَهِّرَكُمْ تَطْهِيرًا. (القرآن الكريم، ٣٣:٣٣)

And stay quietly in your houses, and make not a dazzling display, like that of the former Times of Ignorance; and establish regular Prayer, and give regular Charity; and obey Allah and His Messenger. And Allah only wishes to remove all abomination from you, ye members of the Family, and to make you pure and spotless. (The Qur'an, 33:33)

These verses were revealed to the Prophet by specifically addressing His current five wives as well as His family members—males and females and specifically at a time when the message of Islam was still being formulated. These verses were not addressing all Muslim women. These verses advised the Prophet's family members how to behave as pious Muslims especially during the challenging times of war. Mernissi draws on Al Tabari's interpretation of the above two verses and contextualized their revelation again in year 5 A.H., a particularly challenging military time in Al Medina when the Prophet's family needed more protection. More importantly, they needed to be overly well-behaved and inspiring to other Muslims who were living as immigrants in Al Medina and were still suffering from a military loss (Mernissi, 1991). Though these verses were only referring to the Prophet's wives and were significant to the particular time of their revelation, they were generalized to all Muslim women and extended beyond the beginnings of the Muslim "nation."

Expanding on Mernissi's deconstructive analysis, I deveiled the decontextualized 16 hijab related Qur'anic verses using asbab al nuzul and historical references, and helped illustrate, (1) how these verses have been misinterpreted and overgeneralized to all times and to all Muslim women, (2) how the visual hijab was overemphasized and prioritized over the more called for spiritual hijab, and (3) how modest dress and behavior was only instructed on women and not men too. Such consequences of the deveiling of the verses illustrated how the hijab was reduced to its visual and spatial physical meanings obscuring a main message of Islam, the pursuit of deeper knowledge.

That is, this *deveiling* showed how the *hijab* discourse as a gendering discourse was constructed out of decontextualized and androcentric interpretations of the sacred Qur'anic text and consequently how it disciplined Muslim women's bodies in dress, behavior, and presence in public.

(DE)AUTHENTICATING THE POPULAR MISOGYNISTIC *AHADĪTH*

The second step in *deveiling* the *hijab* discourse and how it came into being, as a gendering discourse, is to (de)authenticate the misogynistic text in the Hadīth, another canonical text beside the Qur'an and *Lisan Al 'Arab*. The Hadīth or *ahadīth* are "sayings attributed to the Prophet Mohamed" (Badran 2009, p. 234) or the oral reports of Prophet Mohammed's teachings and practices (Clarke, 2003; Mernissi, 1991), or the "reports of incidents in which the Prophet Muhammad said or did something that was observed by his followers and passed on orally until later written down" (Kugle, 2010, p. 73). The Hadīth, the secondary Islamic sacred text or the primary Islamic text after the Qur'an, have become the reference that serves to establish the exemplary pattern (*Sunnah*) of the Prophet's life that guides and teaches the believers in their behavior and daily life (Clarke, 2003; Kugle, 2010; Mernissi, 1991). The Hadīth or *ahadīth* are often called "traditions" or *al turath*, heritage, social norms, social expectations (Kugle, 2010).

For the purpose of *deveiling* the *hijab* discourse, I draw on Mernissi's (1991) deconstruction of the misogynistic text in the Hadīth, and particularly her (de)authenticating work of one very popular misogynistic *hadīth*, the *falah ahadīth*,

[8] لن يفلح قوم ولوا أمرهم امرأة. (صحيح البخاري)

> Those who entrust their affairs to a woman will never know prosperity [falah] [or victory or attain/gian Heaven]. (Sahih Al Bukhari, Mernissi, 1991, p. 49)

The *falah hadīth*, among many popular misogynistic *ahadīth*, had played a significant role in reinforcing the (de)contextualized interpretations of the *hijabs* Qur'anic verses, that constituted women as a problem, and thus, enabling the gendering *hijab* discourse. Before going to the specifics of this misogynistic hadīth and how Mernissi (de)authenticated it, I will discuss the classical Islamic methods of scrutinizing the trustworthiness of a *hadīth*

Using the Classical Islamic Tools of Scrutinizing the Authenticity of the *Hadīth*

Scholars used two supplementary classical Islamic methods of testing the authenticity of *hadīth* transcription/textual documentation—*isnad* (reliability) and *matn* (validity). First, *isnad* is the method of establishing the "reliability of the individual oral reports according to a graded scale, ranging from 'attested by several trustworthy authorities' to 'forged' (Clarke, 2003, p. 249). Additionally, Mernissi explained that *isnad* is the method of authenticating the transmission chain or

> the chain of people who transmitted it [the *hadīth*] for its source, its source being a Companion of the Prophet when it has heard it said or seen it done. A Companion might be a man or a woman, a prominent person or a slave. The important points were that person's proximity to the Prophet, his or her personal qualities, and especially the reputation for having a good memory and for not recounting just anything. (1991, p. 35)

Scholars triangulated *isnad's* five tools that result in classifying the degree of the *hadīth's* authenticity as *sahih*, reliable or "deemed not ultimately confirmed but good enough to use" (Kugle, 2010, p. 80). As a result, they categorized a *hadīth* as *maqbul*, acceptable, *hasan*, good enough, *da'if*, weak or defective, *mardud*, rejected, *mushtabah*, suspected, or *mawdu'*, fabricated (Mernissi, 1991; Kugle, 2010). It is worth emphasizing that by applying at least the rigorous *isnad* tools of authenticating a *hadīth*, Kugle (2010) argued that only "about 78 *hadīth* reports reach the rare [highest] quality of reliability called *mutawatir* ... "continuously narrated" (p. 79). This means that this kind of authenticated *ahadīth*, *mutawatir*, the most valuable kind of *hadīth*, are rare. Moreover, those *ahadīth* classified strong and authentic and may have become canonized without further questioning, and according to Kugle, "they were never considered unassailable or inerrant" (2010, p. 78).

Additionally, the enormous number of those *ahadīth* that were classified as less than strong or not *mutawatir* continued to circulate, and thus, built and reinforced opinions perpetuating already-established normative discourses (Kugle, 2010; Mernissi, 1991). Popular *ahadīth* are thus not necessarily those that are authenticated and are only accessible out of "a vast literature written in antique Arabic" (Clarke, 2003, p. 248). Kugle (2010) further explained how unauthenticated *ahadīth* have become popular,

> Muslims must admit that classical categories were codified and critical techniques were defined long after the hadith were in wide circulation, first orally and then in written form. We must not imagine that these texts preexisted the reports being tested or that these categories prevented weak hadith from circulating widely. (p. 83)

Second, the *matn*, or *matn* criticism, is the method by which the validity of information conveyed in a *hadīth* is assessed and questioned (Kugle, 2010). Though in the classical Islamic methodologies, *matn* is secondary to *isnad* and it may be supplementary to its conclusions, it may also reject a *hadīth* as "inauthentic even if its *isnad* is plausible" (Kugle, 2003, p. 81). Scholars are currently using *matn* criticism to verify a *hadīth* by asking, "whether the report's *matn* contain information that goes against common experience, scientific observation, medical knowledge, or historical and geographical facts" (Kugle, 2010, p. 81). Moreover, scholars apply *matn* criticisms by doing a sociological analysis or

> examining the specificity of matn.... Does it relay information in the context of an actual event in the life of the Prophet, rather than a judicial decision that is devoid of context? This was not a technique that was used in the classical times, but modern scholars maintain its usefulness. We know much about the Prophets and his companions through other genres of Islamic literature. In roughly the same era that the hadith were being compiled, other authors were recording events of the Prophet's life ... comparing the hadith with other accounts of the Prophet's life can thus help us to reconstruct the context of the information conveyed by reports, a content the hadith format tend to strip away. (Kugle, 2003, p. 81)

Scholars are also using *matn* criticisms to verify a *hadīth* by doing a linguistic analysis, or to ask, "whether the speech that the report attributed to Prophet did not or could not have used. If they did, they were rejected as fabrications even if they had a plausible *isnad* (Kugle, 2003, p. 81). Given the use of language at a particular era, the timing of the assembly of the *ahadīth* in books—the historical context—and the positionalities of the scholars authenticating them, make authentication of a *hadīth* an interpretive task open to suspicion or calls for scrutiny especially in relation to gender and sexuality (Kugle, 2010). Thus, many critical Muslim scholars of this time are questioning a number of *ahadīth* by examining their *isnad* and *matn* together (Ali, 2006; Clarke, 2003; Kugle, 2010; Mernissi, 1991). That is, they examine who uttered them, where, when, why, to whom and how do they work against current sociological theories and understandings of gender and sexuality. More specifically, the multiple methods of authenticating a *hadīth* have become more widely used by progressive and libratory Islamic studies scholars, like Scott Siraji al-Haqq Kugle (2010) who in his most recent and very illuminating work on homosexuality in Islam explains,

> There is a high probability that a report with a matn stripped of contextual information and with solitary isnad is of this type [acceptable, good enough, defective, rejected, suspected, or fabricated], which reflects the folk wisdom or common opinion of members of the Muslim community in later generations rather than the words of the Prophet himself. (p. 83)

In order to understand how some inauthentic *ahadīth* had the power to contribute to an almost two-millennia old gendering discourse inscribing *muslimat's* bodies, *arab-muslim* and Islamic feminist scholars had to take the urgent task of directly turning to the Hadīth text by using the multiple classical Islamic methods of *isnad* and *matn* (Ahmed, 1992; Badran, 2009; El Saadawi, 1998; Mernissi, 1991).

Mernissi had selected the misogynistic infamous *falah hadīth* to expose how with other unauthenticated *ahadīth* it "shored patriarchal ideas and practices" (Badran, 2009, p. 247), and thus, cultivated the grounds for a gendering discourse. Mernissi exposed the *falah hadīth* misogynistic effect not only because Abu Bakra—the Prophet's companion and renowned credible reporter of the Hadīth—transmitted it as an authentic *hadīth* but also because Abu Bakra recollected it and used it in a very specific circumstance. First, Mernissi used *isnad* to verify the credibility of the chain of narration transmitting a *hadīth* leading back to the Prophet. This included a check on the "morality of the narrators to judge whether they are believers in Islam, not biased by heresy or sectarian partisanship, and liars" (Kugle, 2010, p. 79). Particularly, Mernissi used *isnad* not only to check on the reliability of the narrators in general but more specifically to check on the narrator's gender predispositions.

To embark on this huge first step, Mernissi thoroughly reviewed Sahih, a major and canonized reference that includes thousands of authenticated *ahadīth* accepted by the meticulous scholar Al Bukhari (194-256 A.H.). Importantly, Mernissi noted that Al Bukhari's use of *isnad* allowed him to retain "as authentic only 7,257 Hadith … when there were already 596,725 false Hadith in circulation" (p. 44) and that his work was completed less than two centuries after the death of the Prophet. Mernissi was suspicious of these few remaining *ahadīth* in Sahih Al Bukhari—authenticated only by using *isnad*—because they were reported and circulated as "a priori considered true and therefore unassailable without proof for the contrary" (1991, p. 49). She insisted that nothing bans her "as a Muslim woman, from making a double investigation—historical and methodological—of [the] Hadith and its author, and especially the condition in which it was first put to use" (1991, p. 49). By doing a double investigation, Mernissi was not challenging Al Bukhari's ethical stands and meticulous work but she was extending his work by drawing on the later and more refined work of Ibn Hajar Al 'Asqalani (773-852), mainly commenting on Al Bukhari's work. In other words, Mernissi opted to use *matn* along with *isnad* to test the authenticity of the misogynistic *falah hadīth*.

To do this double investigation, Mernissi used *matn* as a method to verify the validity of the information relayed in the *falah hadīth* (Mernissi, 1991; Kugle, 2010). She checked the robustness of the information in the *hadīth* in three ways, (1) she exposed the *zarf al-riwayah*, or the historical, geographical, and sociological contexts in which the reporting occurred (Abu El Fadl, 2001; Mernissi, 1991), (2) she conducted a linguistic analysis, and (c) she checked the *hadīth's* consistency with current "scientific observations and medical knowledge" (Kugle, 2010, p. 81).

Triangulating the results of both *isnad* and *matn*, Mernissi courageously questioned the authenticity of *falah* misogynistic *hadīth* and showed how it has been widely circulated and thus, cultivating the grounds for a gendering discourse. To do so, Mernissi (1991) scrutinized and (de)authenticated one very popular misogynistic *hadīth*, or what I refer to from here on as the *falah hadīth* (Sahih Al Bukhari, *hadīth* 7099), by taking three steps. One, she exposed the historical and patriarchal social context in which *falah* misogynistic *hadīth* was first recollected. That is, she used *zarf al-riwayah*, or the historical, geographical, and sociological contexts in which the reporting occurred (Abu El Fadl, 2001; Mernissi, 1991). Two, she exposed the credibility and androcenticity of the *hadīth*'s narrator. Third, she conducted a linguistic analysis. Fourth, she checked the *hadīth*'s consistency with current "scientific observations and medical knowledge" (Kugle, 2010, p. 81).

Historicizing the Misogynistic *Ahadīth*

Mernissi used *matn* as a first step to (de)authenticate a bluntly misogynistic and widely circulated *hadīth*, the *falah hadīth* (Sahih Al Bukhari, *hadīth* 7099). She went beyond Al Bukhari reporting the content of the *falah* misogynistic *hadīth* and exposed the historical and patriarchal social context in which, (1) the Prophet is supposed to have uttered it, and (2) Abu Bakra decided to recollect it and use it. Mernissi (1991) drew on Al 'Asqalani's extensive work in which he described, "the political events that served as background, a description of the battles, the identity of the conflicting parties" (Mernissi, 1991, p. 50).

First, to historicize the *falah hadīth* Mernissi exposed how the Prophet supposedly uttered this *hadīth* when He learned that the Persians named a woman to rule them in place of her assassinated father, Kisra, the King of the Sassanid Empire (Mernissi, 1991). This was a time (A.D. 628) of endless wars between the Romans and the Persians. Of course, intrigued by the news the Prophet asked, "'And who had replaced him in command?' The answer was: 'They have entrusted power to his daughter'" (Mernissi, 1991, p. 49).

Mernissi argues that this *hadīth* could not be referring to *muslim* women or all women but to a specific Persian empress as she questions, "Could this be the incident that led the Prophet to pronounce this *hadīth* against women?" (1991, p. 50) Mernissi goes on to argue when this *hadīth* is contextualized, the Prophet may have been wishing the Persians as a powerful empire of the time to "never know prosperity or victory [falah]." In other words, as the Prophet was following the development of the wars between two current powers close to Arabia, the Romans and the Persian, He was wishing that they fail or not prosper since he was anticipating Muslims would have to confront them sooner or later (Mernissi, 1991).

Moreover, if falah (root verb flh) in this hadīth meant "attaining/gaining Heaven" (Lisan Al 'Arab) then the Prophet may have been referring to the new Persian empress as somebody who cannot gain the reward of Heaven because she simply was not Muslim. The Prophet may have also been also referring to the Persians—who were not Muslims at the time—as people who could not "attain/gain Heaven" because they were not being lead by a Muslim woman. This hadīth, may also be reflecting the Prophet's ambition in spreading His message of Islam after the collapse of the Roman and Persian powers to the people who are not Muslims yet or to those who are eligible to attain Heaven, whether lead by men or women.

In the contextualized and nonandocentric possible meanings above, Mernissi (1991) asserted that Abu Bakra recollected a hadīth in which the Prophet could not have been referring to Muslim women or to all women as incapable of leadership nor was He excluding Muslim women altogether from political leadership.

With this scrutiny, Mernissi (1991) was showing how Abu Bakra's timing of the reporting stripped of its historical context but reflective of andocentric connotations normalized the notion that those who are ruled by a woman will not gain the promise of paradise. In other words, women who are unable to lead people successfully, should not be governing Muslims or a nation, or should not be part of public life because they will lead Muslims or people away from paradise.

Second, to further historicize the falah hadīth (Sahih Al Bukhari, hadīth 7099), Mernissi exposed how Abu Bakra chose to report it not only 25 years after the death of the Prophet but also at a time of potential fitnah.[9] The Arabic noun fitnah is derived from the root verb ftn. According to Lisan Al 'Arab, ftn means to burn, kill, and fight. Ftn also means to test and differentiate between the good and the bad, or to have a difference in opinion. Moreover, it means to get lost to the evil way or avert from the truth and Paradise, deceive like the devil, sin and commit a crime, not to believe in Allah, be mentally incapable or deranged. Significantly, ftn means to tempt or seduce—mainly women to men—and to be infatuated—mainly men by women (Lisan Al 'Arab). Moreover, Clarke emphasized that fitnah is the "dangerous feminine" or "the danger to men and society of temptations posed by women and by women's own nature and desires" (2003, p. 251). Additionally, Badran (2009) added that notions of women as an "omnisexual—highly sexualized" is a way of thinking shared by both Christians and Muslims, who generally believe that women's sexuality, is the product of "nature." Women, as omnisexual creatures, have been associated with disorder or chaos (fitna) connected with sexuality, and, as Mernissi reminds us, a beautiful woman may be called fitna (as femme fetal). Women must be contained, therefore, to preserve social order. (p. 171)

That is, Abu Bakra chose to report the *falah hadīth* (Sahih Al Bukhari, *hadīth* 7099), at a time when the Muslims fought amongst themselves in the controversial Camel battle, "the first in which Muslims shed Muslim blood" (Ahmed, 1992, p. 61). It was a crucial time of political struggle between two very intelligent leaders and faithful followers of the Prophet, one who happened to be a woman, the mother of all the believers, and the most beloved wife to the Prophet. Abu Bakra's reporting was conveniently made when the third caliph 'Uthman was assassinated and the Muslims including 'Aisha were calling 'Ali, the fourth caliph, to bring the murderers to justice (Mernissi, 1991). This meant that 'Aisha with her followers was in conflict with 'Ali over the priorities and ways of governance of the Muslims. 'Aisha disagreement with 'Ali led to a divided public opinion, that is, should a Muslim submit to an unjust caliph—'Ali—(who did not punish the killers of 'Uthman) or rebel against him and call for justice with 'Aisha (Mernissi, 1991). Mernissi further explained,

> For those who held the first opinion, the gravest danger that the Muslim nation could face was not that of being ruled by an unjust leader, but rather of falling into civil war. Let us not forget that the word Islam means submission. If the leader was challenged, the fundamental principle of Islam as order was in danger. The others thought that the lack of justice of the Muslim chief of state was more serious than civil war. A Mulsim must not turn his back when he sees his leader commit injustice and reprehensible act. (Mernissi, 1991, p. 55)

At this time, 'Aisha was more concerned about strengthening justice and setting its practices among the Muslim caliphs. She was more concerned about peaceful negotiations of democratic governance that would assure unity and stability in the young Muslim nation (Mernissi, 1991). With this in the background, Mernissi argued that "by the fact that one of the parties [in this conflict] is a woman" (1991, p. 57) and the timing of Abu Bakra's recollecting the *falah hadīth* (Sahih Al Bukhari, *hadīth* 7099) reflected his gender-biased position. This battle started with 'Aisha's opposition of 'Ali's succession as the fourth caliph, "gave rise eventually to the split between Sunni and Shiite Muslims (Ahmed, 1992, p. 61), and more importantly 'Aisha lost it.

Mernissi argued that *fitn* strong linguistic link between the negative meanings and women and Abu Bakra's timing of recollection of the *falah hadīth* normalized two devastating constructions of women. The meaning and the recollecting this unauthenticated words of the Prophet at a time of loss and fighting among Muslims with 'Aisha leading opposition to the caliph, certainly helped to construct women as unable or unworthy of trust to lead and govern Muslims, and more alarmingly, as the instigation source and cause of dire strife to Muslims (Mernissi, 1991). Abu Bakra was able by reporting the *falah hadīth* to construct 'Aisha, a female leader, as an incapable leader and an instigator and igniter of the worst possible situation, the fighting amongst Muslims (chaos), a big sin the Prophet warned the Muslim to avoid.

The power of prevalent language and Abu Bakra's use of the sacred word of the Prophet are clear reflections of the misogynistic intention of Abu Bakra and his patriarchal time—an extension of the pre-Islamic era (Ahmed, 1992). This is how the *falah hadīth* became very popular and has deeply established *muslimah* as a *problem* to fear, discipline, containment, protection, and control in public spaces and political realms (Ahmed, 1992; Mernissi, 1991).

Furthermore, to substantiate the (de)authentication of the *falah* misogynistic *hadīth* historicizing its recollection during the period of fighting amongst Muslims, Mernissi moved next to assess this *hadīth* according to the credibility of its reporter, Abu Bakra.

Scrutinizing the Credibility of the *Ahadīth* Narrators

In the second step of (de)authenticating the bluntly misogynistic and widely circulated *falah hadīth*, Mernissi exposed and questioned the credibility of its reporter, Abu Bakra. To further disqualify Abu Bakra's credibility as a *hadīth* reporter, Mernissi drew on the work of Malik Ibn Anas (93-179 A.H.), one of the most famous imams of Islam who asserted the moral criteria of those who could transmit a *hadīth*. Mernissi followed the advice of Ibn Anas that every Muslim should direct his/her "suspicion at the transmitters" … emphasis on "the necessity to be on their guard" … and to "take the daily behavior of sources into consideration as a criterion for their reliability" (1991, p. 60).

By applying Ibn Anas' advice to be critical of the *hadīth* transmitters, Mernissi writes, "he [Abu Bakra] would have to be immediately eliminated, since one of the biographies of time tells us that he was convicted and flogged for false testimony by the caliph 'Umar Ibn al-Khattab [second caliph]" (1991, p. 60). With such a precedent and according to Ibn Anas' moral principle qualifying a *hadīth* transmitter, Mernissi ends her scrutiny of Abu Bakra by writing, "Abu Bakra must be rejected as a source of Hadith" (1991, p. 61).

Additionally, she drew on the huge work of Al 'Asqalani that went into details of "the identity of the transmitters and their opinions, and finally the debates [of the time] concerning their reliability" (Mernissi, 1991, p. 50). She exposed Abu Bakra's social and political trajectory, his tendency to make up stories and reports, many of which were reflective of his androcentric stand against 'Aisha's political leadership who was calling for justice at the early makings of the nation of Islam. Mernissi described who Abu Bakra was, how he came to Islam and how he gained his status social and political from being a slave to becoming a part of the ruling elite. Answering the call of the Prophet after the siege of Ta'if (8 A.H.), Abu Bakra converted to Islam, and was immediately freed from slavery. Mernissi explains, "since his conversion Abu Bakra had scaled the social ladder at a dizzying pace" (p. 51). His paternity was not traceable, a criteria significant to Muslim society at the time and reflective of higher social status. That is, recently freed from slavery and with no traceable paternity, Abu Bakra may have been socially vulnerable at time but "Islam had given [him] not only fortune and prestige, but, still more important, an [religious] identity" (Mernissi, 1991, p. 53). In this Mernissi (1991) argues that it is easy to imagine that Abu Bakra "was the enemy of any civil war that could undermine the establishing of Muslim society" (p. 53) that gave him status. In other words, Abu Bakra had at least a personal motive in bringing up both the *falah* misogynistic *hadīth* at a time suitable to justify and solidify his political ambitions in siding with 'Ali who later appointed him as his governor in Basra.

Exposing the historical and patriarchal social context in which *falah* misogynistic *hadīth* was first recollected, the credibility and androcenticity of the *hadīth* narrator, andocentric popular meanings of *falah*, and inconsistency of gender construction with current knowledge, Mernissi concluded her work on (de)authenticating the misogynist *hadīth*. She claimed as a result that the circulation of the *falah hadīth* at a *fitnah* period along with many popular misogynistic *hadīth* undoubtedly reinforced the (de)contextualized meanings of the *hijabs* in the Qur'anic verses. These popularized interpretations of the related *hijab* Qur'anic verses and the overused misogynistic *hadīth* were major contributors to construction as well as the sustenance of the *hijab* discourse itself.[10]

ENABLING A GENDERING DISCOURSE

Expanding on Mernissi and Clarke's deconstructive analysis of the canonical texts of *Lisan Al 'Arab*, the Quran, and the Hadīth, I have deveiled how a gendering discourse, the *hijab* discourse, was hegemonized. *Deveiling* of the *hijab* Qur'anic verses and (de)authenticating a major misogynistic *hadīth*, I reframed the extensive deconstructive analysis and groundbreaking *ijtihad* of Linda Clarke (2003), Scott Siraji al-Haqq Kugle (2010) and Fatima Mernissi (1991). These scholars used the classical Islamic research tools to directly access the text that became the "source of law and the standard [shaping] Muslim ethics and values" (Mernissi, 1991, p. 1). These scholars particularly used philological and interpretive methodologies of exegesis, *tafsir*. First, they expanded the use of the classical tools of interpretations such as *asbab al nuzul* to expose the decontextualized and dehistoricized the popular gendering interpretations of the written *text* of the Qur'an. Second, they triangulated the multiple tools of *isnad* (reliability) and *matn* (validity) to expose the lack of authenticity of the spoken major misogynistic *hadīth*.

That is, Mernissi and Clarke accomplished the difficult tasks of *deveiling* or of textual interpretation of the Qur'an and authentication of the Hadīth without mediation. By taking the task of rereading the *text* directly, these scholars pursued the first revelation and first order of Allah to Mohammed in the Qur'anic verse (96:1), "Read in the name of your God Who created (Mernissi, 1991). To Margot Badran (2009) this process of *deveiling* is "gendered *ijtihad*," a "methodology that feminist and Islamist women have used to reread the Qur'an and other religious texts to expose patriarchal interpretations and to advance more gender-just understandings of Islam" (2009, p. 232). Moreover, this *deveiling* process informed the methodology of this study, as shown in Chapters 3, 4, and 5; and led me to my vision of *deveiling* pedagogies, as discussed in Chapter 6.

Deveiling the *hijab* discourse was possible first by deconstructing the *hijabs* in the relevant Qur'anic verses, and second, by (de)authenticating a major popular misogynistic *hadīth*. It is the process of expanding the *hijabs'* reduced linguistic scope in Arabic and exposing their decontextualized interpretations. It is the process of exposing the hidden hegemony embedded in the written language as well as in the orally transmitted decontextualized interpretations of the Qur'anic verses and the supposedly authenticated Hadīth reportings. More importantly, this *deveiling* process exposed the androcentric positionalities of those who constructed and normalized these popularized meanings and the encouraging patriarchal social conditions of the shifting moments of the foundation of the Muslim nation. In other words, this process of *deveiling* exposed how the values and practices promoted in the decontextualized and reduced meanings of the *hijab* as well as the popularized unauthentic and misogynistic *ahadīth* have come to comprise "ideas, ideologies, and referents, that systematically construct both the subjects [Muslim females] and objects [bodies of Muslim females] of which they speak," and thus have constructed a gendering discourse "integral to the construction of the social reality" (Hesse-Biber & Leavy, 2006, p. 293) of Muslim females.

First, Mernissi's deconstructive analysis using the philological interpretive methodology challenged the assumptions that there is only one meaning to the *hijab* or that the *hijab* is only confined to its physical dimension in the visual and the spatial. Mernissi showed that the main Arab dictionary's linguistic emphasis only on the *hijab*'s two physical and visible meanings is reflected in the taken-for-granted interpretations of the most circulated *hijab* Qur'anic verses (The Qur'an, 24:31; 33:53). These verses emphasize only the visual and spatial dimensions of the *hijab*. The classical and commonly adopted interpretations of these verses dismissed the other overlapping ethical and invisible *hijabs*. That is, the emphasis of both the Arab dictionary and the popularized interpretations of the two major *hijab* verses limited and simplified the *hijabs'* linguistic scope to only its physical—visual and spatial. That is, this emphasis fixed the *hijab* reference to a material tool that systematically constructed the *muslimah's* body as an *object* to be protected through her dress and movement especially in public. Simultaneously, hiding the *hijabs'* dynamic ethical and spiritual dimensions hindered the possibilities for the *muslimah* to express her body—in dress and presence and behavior in public—in dynamic and fluid ways. Thus, the dominance of the fixed physical meaning of the *hijab* closed off and displaced its more desirable multiple and fluid meanings in the lives of Muslims. This kind of censorship set the linguistic conditions necessary to systemize the objectification of women, and thus, construct a discourse that specifically hegemonized the *muslimah's* body (Hesse-Biber & Leavy, 2006).

In the same trend, emphasizing the physical dimensions of the *hijab* and obstructing its spiritual dimension in the 16 *hijab*-related Qur'anic verses, normalized its visual and spatial dimensions, and thus, limited more fluid and expandable meanings. As such, the *hijab*'s visual and spatial values have become more entrenched in the popular meanings of the *hijab*, and thus, its common sensical/taken-for-granted practices—focusing on dressing women and secluding them from the public arena. Additionally, in this process reducing and normalizing the *hijab* to its physical meaning, Muslims in general and Muslim women specifically have become easily distracted from the more reiterated Qur'anic references of the spiritual *hijab* and thus its importance to their multiple and fluid *muslimness*.

Moreover, decontextualizing the Qur'anic interpretations of the most popular and major *hijab*-related verses (33:53 and 33:59) authorized the control of the *muslimah's* body through her dress and mobility in public. The decontextualized interpretations of the most sacred Islamic text guarded by androcentric obstructed from reading the text directly and scholars, was another covert censorship tactic that helped to normalize and hegemonize the limited values and practices of the *hijab*. Keeping the Qur'an's interpretations away from the populous, especially women, eventually normalized the *hijabs* to become a gendering discourse. Additionally, cultivating conditions that do not allow the questioning of authority hegemonized a discourse that became very difficult to challenge and interrupt. In other words, the fixation on the physical *hijabs* as well as keeping the Islamic fundamental texts inaccessible, and thus, unquestioned for too long (Ahmed, 1992; Mernissi, 1991), have succeeded in creating complex interconnected webs of values and practices (Hesse-Biber, 2007), unsurprisingly enabling the *hijab* as a gendering discourse.

The control of meaning in language confined the *hijab* in just one or two isolated citations in the most sacred Islamic text, the Qur'an and located it "in institutions and practices, which define difference and shape the material world, [mainly and specifically] including bodies" (Weedon, 1999, p. 103) of *muslimat*. Controlling language by limiting the circulation of the multiplicity of a meaning and monopolizing access to tools of knowing and interpreting alternatively and critically are covert strategies that limited the possibilities of interrupting the normativity of the *hijab*. These strategies displaced its multiple and shifting meanings outside the Muslim women's lived experiences. With the persistence of these strategies, Muslims were obstructed from reading the text directly and were more dependent on the androcentric readings of the text. As such, this covert strategy of hegemonizing the meaning of the *hijab*—linguistically and Qur'anically—has constructed its normativity through covert and noncoercive tools regulating the *muslimah's* body. With control of language, a gendering discourse was socially constructed and maintained by displacing the *hijab's* multiplicity out of the popular linguistic use and decontextualizing its references in Qur'an and the Hadīth.

Second, Mernissi showed how the *falah* misogynistic *hadīth* prompted a normative meaning about the inability of women to lead the nation and her danger in instigating disorder in the society. This slippage of meaning helped support the above tactics of controlling the fixed *hijab* meaning and the construction of women as a threat and a problem to the nation of Islam, and thus, harbored gendering discourses that at least discourage Muslim women participating in the political arena. Such popular and misogynistic *hadīth* constructed the norms in which women became easily excluded from decision making and from politics.

Additionally, the timing of collecting the Hadīth years after the death of the Prophet meant that many *ahadīth* were already circulating among Muslims "as they are," decontextualized and dehistoricized. More importantly many of the *ahadīth* that were not so strongly reliable, or highly authenticated, have carried with them the misogynistic message and the narrators' androcentric standpoints who were still living and holding on to the patriarchal privileges inherited from the pre-Islamic era. The inaccessibility of the classical Islamic interpretive tools to the public especially women and the ease of oral transmission of the *ahadīth* resulted in maintaining the practice of not questioning the credibility of the *ahadīth* narrators but also reinforced their ability and authority to circulate misogynistic messages as Islamic norms to seclude Muslim women from the public reach and realm of men.

The traditional scholars of the time used the orally and easily circulated weak or not highly authenticated *ahadīth* together with the Qur'an to arrive at major legal jurisprudence rulings that established societal norms. These rulings and norms also have not escaped the gender-biased attitudes and male-dominated political manipulations that were prevalent not only during the life of the Prophet but also during the time the Hadīth was fully recorded and interpreted in classical Islamic literature (Abu El Fadl, 2001; Clarke, 2003; Kugle, 2010; Mernissi, 1991). That is, given that the *hijab* Qur'anic verse and *ahadīth* were merely interpreted and reported by male elite of the time with the exception of 'Aisha, critical *arab-muslim* and Islamic feminists assert that both the *hijab* verses and misogynistic *ahadīth* became the tools to "shore up patriarchal ideas and practices" (Badran, 2009, p. 247). Most of the popularized reportings of and interpretations of the weak *ahadīth* reflected the dominant discourses of the time, including homophobic and sexist discourses (Kugle, 2010).

Moreover, the prolonged ignorance of the ability to cross the spiritual *hijab* and the unauthenticity of the misogynistic *ahadīth*, and more importantly the underuse of the Islamic critical tools of research and learning have successfully contributed in hegemonizing the *hijab* discourse in the *Muslimat's* lives (Mernissi, 1991). Such conditions have made the possibilities of challenging the *hijabs* normative effects unimaginable. However, I must add here that drawing and adding on Clarke's and Mernissi's work, it is very possible to surpass the patriarchal male elite scholars who withhold the unquestionable meanings of the sacred texts from the general public and from Muslim women particularly (Mernissi, 1991). It is possible for Muslims to engage in the (re)interpretations of the Qur'an and the authentication of the Hadīth without a mediator (Barazangi, 2009; Wadud, 1999). That is, appropriating the Islamic research methods with a critical feminist epistemology, the *hijab* discourse is exposable as a regulating system that produces knowledge within certain constraints or rules that seem too hard to think beyond and critique (Said, 1979). More excitingly at the same time, this exposability of the *hijab* discourse opens the possibilities for the *muslimat* to participate themselves in its critique and interruption.

Moreover, the traditional scholars of the time used the supposedly authenticated remaining collection of the *ahadīth* together with the Qur'an to arrive to major legal jurisprudence rulings or more societal norms. These rulings and norms also have not escaped the gender-biased attitudes and male-dominated political manipulations that were prevalent not only during the life of the Prophet but also during the time the Hadīth was fully recorded and interpreted in classical Islamic literature (Abu El Fadl, 2001; Clarke, 2003; Kugle, 2010; Mernissi, 1991).

The results of this *deveiling* showed that the interaction between the decontextualized and reduced meanings of the *hijabs* in the Qur'an and the unauthenticated popular misogynistic *ahadīth* covertly normalized the controlling of *muslimah's* body in dress and in mobility and limited her contribution to the public realm. In other words, these *ahadīth* with the implication of their androcentric intentions normalized the *hijabs* as the tool of seclusion and exclusion of women from the public realm. More importantly, these *hijabs* were the tools that closed the possibilities to contemplate the idea of entrusting the *muslimat* in public affairs thus their ability or legitimacy in leading group prayers or leading and governing the *muslims*.

SUMMARY

In this chapter, I have deveiled how a gendering discourse, the *hijab* discourse, was socially constructed and became central to the lives of all kinds of *muslimat—muslim* females. I expanded on the deconstructive analysis Mernissi (1991) and Clarke (2003) of the canonical texts of *Lisan Al 'Arab*, the Qur'an and the Hadīth.

What follows is a discussion of how Mernissi's conceptualization of the *hijabs* and the exposure of a gendering discourse both framed the methodology of this study.

CHAPTER 3

A *DEVEILING* METHODOLOGY

Methods are simply research techniques, tools that get at the research problem, whereas epistemology shapes our research questions and the theories we hold about the social world. Methodology can be thought of as a bridge between epistemology and method, shaping how we approach and conduct research. Whether one's epistemology is rooted in empiricism, standpoint, postmodernism, or postcolonial critique, feminist methodology challenges status quo forms of research by linking theory and method in a synergistic relationship that brings epistemology, methodology, and method into dynamic interaction across the research process. A feminist methodology can spawn the development of new methodological tools that in turn offer new angles of vision, reshaping both our research questions and the way we build knowledge. (Hesse-Biber & Piatelli, 2007, p. 143)

This chapter maps the feminist *deveiling* methodology that guided the 14-month study in which I sought to understand how four Muslim girls, Layla, Dojua, Abby, and Amy, negotiated the *hijab* discourse in the two southwestern U.S. border towns of Al Hilal and Al Jiser. The methodology was a collaborative project framed by a critical feminist approach to qualitative research (Hesse-Biber & Leavy, 2007; Lather, 2007). The collaboration was between four Muslim girls, Layla, Dojua, Abby, and Amy, and one *arabyyah-muslimah* researcher, Manal.

First, I discuss how I worked *with* Layla, Dojua, Abby, and Amy and their parents, constantly negotiating the challenges and complexities that collaborative work brings across differences in language, ways of thinking and doing one's *muslimness*, gender, national and geographical locations, education and class (Swarr & Ngar, 2010). Second, with a critical and fem-

Pedagogies of Deveiling: Muslim Girls and the Hijab Discourse,
pp. 49–73
Copyright © 2012 by Information Age Publishing
All rights of reproduction in any form reserved.

inist approach, I drew on Mernissi's (1991) use of classical Islamic interpretive methods, as insider's methods. I also drew heavily on Hesse-Biber and Leavy's (2007) conceptualization of practicing critical self-reflexivity as the tool of staying aware of the above differences and staying into a negotiation mode with all the participants. Reflexivity is the ongoing work of being mindful and respectful to differences in positionalities among all of the participants throughout the process of research (Hesse-Biber & Brooks, 2007).

Additionally, the work of feminist critical theorists committed to social justice like Michelle Fine (2007) and Patti Lather (1986) further informed this study's feminist *deveiling* methodology. That is, I stayed open to considering the use of a range of interactive methods, Fine and McClelland (2007) call "release methods" or "a hybrid of classic and innovative methods designed to invite the unspeakable to be voiced" (Sirin & Fine, 2008, p. 198). A multiple methods approach is encouraged by other critical feminists working with marginalized young people (Oliver, Hamzeh, & McCaughtry, 2009; Oliver & Hamzeh, 2010). Working with these girls, as young people, I used interactive, alternative and multiple methods, hoping to challenge and counter any consequential injustices of normative discourses these girls lived (Cammarota & Fine, 2008; Sirin & Fine, 2008). That is, the use of innovative and multiple insider's methods while maintaining strong reflexivity, helped me approach the purpose of this study, and thus, offer insights about how these four *muslim* girls negotiated the *hijab* discourse.

Using *deveiling* methodology, as the bridge between my standpoint as an *arabyyah-muslimah* feminist and the shaping of the research process and the insights of this writing, I discuss in the following the interaction between the, (1) spatial and relational contexts, (2) data collection and analysis, and (3) insider's multiple methods and critical self-reflexivity.

SPATIAL AND RELATIONAL CONTEXTS

The Locations and Spaces

In the fall of 2005, when I intended to start a pilot study, I had to first find young Muslim girls in one place who were willing to work with me. I ruled out public schools as appropriate sites for the study and decided to go directly to the local mosque. I chose not to exclusively invite Muslim girls from a diverse student population in the cities' public schools of Al Hilal and Al Jiser—which do not have exclusive schools for Muslims like many other big cities in North America at this time. I did not want to point out Muslim girls through contacting local public schools teachers and asking them to select these girls by any means that have the potential of racializing them. I did not want to deal with the subtly charged Islamophobic atmosphere in the United States through the teachers' reactions to introducing the study. Additionally, it was not possible to identify Muslim girls in the local schools' records since *thankfully* students in U.S. public schools—at the time of the study—were not profiled according to their religion/spiritual affiliation or more complex ethnic/national/linguistic identities.

In the previous semester, I learned from a Muslim student, a participant in a different study in one of the elementary schools, that Muslim girls take Arabic and Qur'an lessons on Sunday afternoons at the mosque. This reality and choice presented the mosque, a focal meeting space of the small Muslim community in town, as the only point to begin the process of selecting the site(s) and the participants for my study. Thus, I decided to literally walk in the mosque as a member of the larger community. The teachers I first met there showed their welcome and interest in my study. They immediately asked me to contact the head of the mosque's counsel for official permission before my next visit.

Right away, I phoned the head of the mosque's counsel. I explained the general purpose of the study and my wish to meet the girls in the mosque. He requested a formal letter to present to the council, a group of men who met once every month. Knowing that the council's meeting was a month away and the response could take some time and some following up, I asked the head of the council to allow me in the mosque premises for warm-up visits until the council members met and looked into my request. He was welcoming and promised to talk to the teachers there to be open about my visits. From this phone call, I began meeting the girls on the mosque's premise and on an official but temporary basis.

The Women's Quarter at the Local Mosque

For the first 7 months of the project, I, spent time in the women's quarters at one of the two local mosques in this southwestern border city, Al Hilal. This was the only space in which Muslim girls gathered in town. According to the head of the counsel, there were approximately 120 Muslims praying with their families at this mosque. It is a small mosque built with a blend of traditional Islamic design and earthy and adobe-like colors and material. The larger interior area for prayer is designated for men while the smaller back area segregates women and children to conduct their educational and religious activities. The women's quarter has two small classrooms, a small hall for group praying, and restrooms. The two classrooms were carpeted, had children's furniture, and few play material or books.

Early October, 2005, I walked to the back of the mosque's building and came to a closed wooden door with a very small sign saying *masslah al nisa'*, women prayer's area. I knocked, took off my shoes at the door, and stepped into a distinctly gender segregated space hearing in the background Arabic and Qur'anic reciting. Immediately, my anxieties began to surface and it was at this moment, I realized that, in this space, I would be strongly challenged by my differences with the teachers, mothers, and girls while contemplating my memories as a girl and woman in other Muslim contexts in which I lived many years of my life.

After a few visits in January and February of 2006, the local mosque became problematic as the site for the study. At this stage, I was still having warm-up conversations with the girls about the purpose of the study and my interest in their participation in physical activities. I was using popular magazines of music and fitness they selected to help approach the purpose of the study—to understand how Muslim girls negotiated the *hijab* discourse. However, meeting the girls and their mothers on Sundays after their weekly lesson for less than an hour was not enough to get into deeper conversations or to include more than one activity/method. Some of the girls could not spend more time after the official Sunday classes and most of their attendance was inconsistent due to a number of Muslim holidays and conflicting functions at the mosque at this time. Additionally, interruptions by the mothers and teachers came with the territory of working with the girls in one of the only two classrooms in this site. Such condition would not allow the girls to open conversations comfortably and allow me to build a relationship with them on the basis of long and consistent meetings.

By the end of each meeting for seven consecutive Sundays, I was still struggling with the tangible differences between the teachers, mothers, and myself, for example over the certainty of the time the girls could spend independently with me and with other more subtle differences I could not name at the time. Every Sunday, I was leaving the mosque extremely exhausted if not feeling paralyzed and unable to continue the study. Thus, as a researcher, I was realizing that sustaining this state of tension with little room to negotiate would render me unable to conduct a study with full wakefulness, an ethical quality crucial to this kind of relational research (Craig & Huber, 2007). This meant that though the council approved my work with the girls in the mosque, it became necessary to locate an alternative site. I needed to find a site without the constraints the mosque was imposing on the girls and me and on the flow of the study's activities. I needed a space in which the girls would feel invited to participate in several activities for longer periods with fewer constraints on time, and at the same time, feel enabled to critically reflect and freely act on their experiences. Thus, I needed a site that would help me approach the purpose of the study—to understand how they negotiated the *hijab* discourse—more than what the mosque was offering at the time.

The University Activity Center

In the middle of March 2006, my advisor, Kim Oliver, made a timely suggestion, to use the activity center on campus as the alternative site of my study. The activity center is a big two-floor building offering many fitness and sport activities in several small and big spaces opened for students, males and females alike. My advisor made this suggestion because this center is the home of her department, Physical Education, Recreation and Dance, the minor I was pursuing in the doctoral program. More importantly, it is a place that offers diverse options for the girls to experience physical activities they expressed their desire and need for during our time in the mosque.

This suggestion and the nature of the place did not confirm the activity center as the study's site right away. At the beginning, as much as I was excited about the possibilities this place would offer, I stayed concerned. The presence of males and the size of the place and its distance from the girls' houses could deter the mothers from committing. With this perplexity, I still took the chance and I began making the necessary communications to prepare the girls, their families, and the administration on campus to make this shift in location possible.

On April 23, 2006, three girls accompanied with their mothers visited the activity center and met Dr. Kim Oliver. After a tour of the center and a pep talk from Kim, followed by an introductory talk from me, the mothers were encouraged to make a tentative promise allowing me to work with the girls during the summer and the fall. The girls were obviously excited about the possible activities they could participate in to fill their summer.

At this time, my advisor offered the department's study lounge to conduct the tasks of this project. The study lounge is located in the first floor of the activity center next to the indoor basketball courts. It is a closed and safe space that gives the privacy needed especially at the beginning to build trust in each other and learn how to conduct the activities of the project. It is a spacious room with two computers and two printers, chairs, a table, cabinets, a sofa, and a refrigerator. It was a private space where the girls were working in one-on-one tasks as well as group activities. They were listening to their own CDs on the CD player, checking their e-mails and their account web pages of MySpace, drinking sodas and eating, searching the Internet for images used in the study's activities, downloading music to listen to through the computer's speakers, and even at points for doing their online homework. In addition, the room had a big-carpeted floor area where the girls later spread the magazines, images, markers, and photos and worked together to make their body collage and scrapbooks.

Starting June 22nd, the study lounge became the focal site that allowed the girls to spontaneously explore other spaces for playing, exercising, or simply socializing and hanging out. On campus, they mainly spent time together in the weightlifting room, the spinning and aerobics classrooms, the cardio equipment and climbing wall area, the basketball court, and the outdoor and indoor swimming pools. All places on campus were part of the university's activity center. The girls also spent times in several places in Al Hilal and Al Jiser, which either I introduced to them because they had a cultural/ educational atmosphere and/or offered healthy-slow food or because the girls themselves chose for their own reasons—to have fun, to shop, to see friends etc. These places ranged from the movie theater and the shops in the local malls, the schools' football stadium in Al Hilal, the girls' houses in Al Hilal and Al Jiser, one of the parents' restaurant in Al Hilal, and one of the father's clinics.

Having the flexibility to move and drive the girls to all of the above spaces was only possible because friends loaned me their reliable and safe car to use on Saturdays. The car was not only another site in which I spent more time with the girls but it was also a crucial tool in this study. It gave me the opportunity to pick up the girls every Saturday. That is, the girls' consistent weekly presence was not all dependent on the availability of a ride from one of their family members. The car also gave me the flexibility to go with the girls any place that presented itself at any time of the study. The car became a facilitator to experience many places, which were of interest to the girls and were a safe and fun place where they could openly express themselves.

The Main Participants

During the first few visits to the Sunday school at the women' quarters of Al Hilal's mosque, I was hoping to invite a few very young girls between the ages of 7 and 9, who specifically wore a headscarf. My assumption then was that working with the younger girls wearing a headscarf would serve the purpose of my study—to understand how Muslim girls negotiated the *hijab* discourse. However, as I continued to listen to the girls' stories and as soon as one of the first mothers I initially approached refused to include her daughter in the study, I had to question the criteria of selecting only Muslim girls who wear a headscarf. To understand Muslim girls' bodily experiences, I had to intensify my efforts to build relationships with any of the girls who were willing to participate in the study, whether wearing a headscarf or not. In time, I gained the approval of only two mothers in this mosque. Their daughters, Layla and Amy happened to be of an older age, between 12 and 16, and were willing and excited to work with me. In turn, Layla and Amy invited their friends, Dojua and Abby, because they thought they would have more fun together participating in the study.

This process of nonselective sampling or "convenience sampling" (Maxwell, 1996, p. 70) allowed me to work with four girls with diverse Muslim profiles who are living in a particular location in the United States. The resulting small number of the participants also enabled me to spend more time with the girls themselves, to know them better, and to capture more of their lived bodily experiences (Denzin & Lincoln, 2005). As a critical feminist educator, I was not seeking in this study to produce empirical generalizations, rather I was interested in finding an opening for an in-depth understanding of how four Muslim girls negotiated the *hijab* discourse in a particular time and specific location (Hesse-Biber & Leavy, 2007). This is in accordance with critical feminist qualitative research that involves a *small sample* aiming to look at "a 'process' or the 'meanings' individuals attribute to their given social situation, not necessarily to make generalizations ... but to understand how they *experience* being overweight, for example, in a thin culture" (Hesse-Biber, 2007, p. 119). This small and convenient sample may also be considered "purposive sample" accepted or chosen on the basis of this study's purpose as well as on the "consideration of the resources available to the researcher" (Hesse-Biber, 2007, p. 119).

Additionally, as an *arab-muslim* living the systemic racializing discourses and structures of the time, I ruled out public schools as sites for the study. I did not want to make any move that would contribute to racializing the girls in an already charged Islamophobic and anti-Arab atmosphere. I decided to try getting into the local mosque in town instead and work with a smaller group of very diverse *muslim* girls. This decision set me to pursue the study's purpose to understand the complexities of *muslim* girls' lived experiences rather than aspiring for generalizable findings that would perpetuate the "racial thinking" (Razack, 2008) about *muslims* as one homogenous group in the schools of North America, Europe, and Australia.

Moving to work outside the mosque, I ended up collaborating with Layla, Dojua, Abby, and Amy[8]—(ages 14-17). They all considered themselves members of Al Hilal and Al Jiser Muslim communities and believers of "one Allah." Dojua and Amy infrequently prayed five times a day, and Layla prayed "five times a day since she was 6 or 7 years old." They all fasted Ramadan and attended the local mosque occasionally. All of them considered English their first language.

I have extracted most of the following biographical description of Layla, Dojua, Abby, and Amy from the self-mapping questionnaire the girls filled out at the beginning of the study and the introductory conversations we had throughout the study.

> I consider myself more Arab because I practice that way of life more at home I do not consider myself just American you know what I mean. (Layla)

Layla was 17 and a junior in high school. She identified as "Arab" and "Arabian." She said, "My culture is almost my whole way of life." Later she said while laughing that sometimes when she is filling applications she checks the category "White Anglo ...or Caucasian." Layla was born in the United States. She visited Saudi Arabia once. Her father maintains strong ties with his family there but does not hold an American passport. Layla's first language is English and she understands some spoken Saudi-Arabic but hardly understands the Arabic of the Qur'an.

Layla's mother, a White American met her father, a Saudi-Arabian, who was a student in the United States. Layla's mother became Muslim later in life and wears a headscarf. Layla's father was studying computer systems at a community college. Her mother worked as a medical transcriber at the clinic of Amy's father. In the same clinic, Layla worked with her older brother some evenings and weekends. Layla had four older and two younger brothers. Layla had been wearing a headscarf in public since she was 11.

Layla loved listening to music—rap and hip hop—reading magazines, dancing, and spending time with her family. Layla did not participate in any physical activities in school or outside school. She had been very good friends with Dojua since elementary school. They usually met when their mothers' visited each other.

> My race is Algerian and [my] ethnicity is the same. (Dojua)

Dojua was a 17-year-old senior in high school and a freshman taking dentistry classes in the local community college. She identified as "Muslim-Algerian." She was born in Algeria and immigrated to the United States with her family when she was eight. Dojua's first language is English and she understands some spoken Spanish. Algerian-Arabic is the main language spoken at home but Dojua hardly uses it elsewhere. Dojua's family makes frequent communication with their families in Algeria yet have only revisited once since their immigration 9 years ago.

Her parents identified as Algerian-American born in Algeria. Dojua's parents earned bachelor degrees in Algeria and have been running their own restaurant for the past 2 years. Dojua worked with them 5 to 6 evenings a week. Her older sister (21 years old) was a university student and was married to an Algerian Muslim and lived in another U.S. city. Her younger brother was 13 years old. Dojua did not wear the headscarf while her mother and older sister did.

Dojua loved shopping and spending money. She was recently accepted at the local state university in Al Hilal. She planned to attend classes the next fall in the school of nursing in preparation for a master's degree in dentistry. Dojua and Layla have been friends since she moved to Al Hilal.

African American ... yes this is what I put in my college application ... it gives me better opportunities and it's not like I am lying or anything. (Abby)

Abby was a 16-year-old junior in high school. She identified as "Algerian and American [which] makes me African American ... I am Muslim. I speak English, Spanish, and Algerian." Abby was born in the United States. Her parents also identified as Algerian-American born in Algeria.

At home her parents speak Algerian-Arabic and French, yet use English as their public and professional language. Abby's parents keep strong ties with their families in Algeria and in different parts of the United States. They have travelled occasionally to Algeria since their immigration about 16 years ago. Abby's father had a master's degree and was a science curriculum developer/consultant for the Al Jiser school district. Her mother, trained as a dentist in Algeria worked as a dental hygienist. Abby's brother was a freshman in Al Jiser's main university. Abby and her mother did not wear a headscarf.

Abby assisted the athletic trainer of the school's men's sports teams and was the photographer for the school year book. Abby aspires for "a career in the health profession specifically getting a doctorate in athletic training." Abby is very good friends with Dojua.

I am from the province of Punjab in Pakistan, so I am Punjabi. My grandparents [came] from India during the 1947 partition, so my ancestors were Punjabi Indian. (Amy)

Amy was a 14-year-old freshman in high school. She identified as "American-Pakistani/Asian-Pakistani of a Muslim-Pakistani culture." Amy was born in Lahore, Pakistan. She immigrated to the United States with her family when she was a baby. Amy's parents are Pakistani-American born in Punjab, India. Amy's home languages are Punjabi, Urdu, and English. Amy's family still has strong ties to Pakistan and travels there at least once a year. Amy wrote, "my mom takes care of [my] younger siblings, cooks, and she is a very caring mother and was trained in political science." Her father is a neurologist and owned his practice with another Pakistani-American pediatrician in Al Hilal. Amy had one younger brother and two sisters. Amy did not wear a headscarf and her mother wore one "loosely" when she was in public. She wrote, "what makes me Muslim is my faith in one Allah" and "not the scarf."

Amy loved reading Harry Potter books and loved learning about law and politics. She enjoyed listening to classic rock and being physically active. At the time of the study, she was attending Tae Kwon Do classes and was previously doing a lot of swimming. Amy was the youngest in the group and had a sisterly relationship with Dojua and Layla. They usually meet when their mothers visit each other or in school.

Manal

At the time of the study, I was a doctoral student in my early forties. I identified as *arabyyah-muslimah*. Arabic is my *home* language and Islam is my religion by birth. I consider myself very Arab. Though I am fluent in Arabic and English, I still consider Arabic my home language. With the university degrees I earned in the United States, English has become the main tool with which I read and write in the academy. However, I am constantly reading Arabic literature and seeking Arabic sources that help my research. In this, I am still doing the "translation" work necessary to teach and research but also to build and maintain relationships in the academy and outside it. Additionally, I am a hybrid between-borders mestiza (Anzaldúa, 1987). I am a mix of nonnomadic tribal Jordanian, Palestinian, Syrian, Turkish, and Kurdish.

Born and raised in Amman, the capital of the Hashemite Kingdom of Jordan, I lived the privileges of a middle-class family not only possessing formal education but also critical literacies necessary to survive in a deeply colonized and hyper-patriarchal context. My mother has an associate college degree and is a trained nurse. My father is a specialized medical doctor and has been a political and social "activist" and a writer throughout his life.

In the late sixties and seventies, I was educated in a bilingual, private, nationalist, and postcolonial all-girls school in Amman. Established in 1926, this school was originally a missionary British school. Though this school was nationalized in the fifties, it continued much of the colonial ways of teaching by specifically privileging English over Arabic. At the same time, the school's formal mission was to prepare Arab women as leaders enabled to build an independent nation resisting colonizing hegemonies.

At age 17, I moved to Washington, DC, and earned two graduate degrees (1979-1986). I returned to Jordan and pioneered a 17-year long career in educational audiology in Jordan, Palestine, and neighboring Arab countries. This career was juxtaposed with activism in Arab-

Jordanian women and deaf affinities (1986-2003). With the peaking of the imperial and colonial wars first in October 2000, I had to (re)cross the Jordan River from Jerusalem to Amman, and then in March 2003, I chose to exile myself out of Jordan.

I was an athlete who played on Jordanian national basketball teams and on U.S. university varsity teams. I have been physically active all my life. At this time, I swim, do yoga, bike, and walk regularly to keep myself physically fit.

I lived most of my life in contexts in which I was constantly negotiating the *hijab* discourse at the intersections of being an athlete and physically active, public professional/figure, crossing classes, and out queer. My name, historical/cultural/linguistic literacies of Arabic, Islam, *muslims*, and the *hijabs* positioned me as an insider (Anzaldúa, 1987; Mohanty, 2003). My nonembodiment of the visible *hijabs* positioned me as an in-between (Anzaldúa, 1987; Mohanty, 2003) with the participants' ways of doing their *muslimness*. Moreover, not being involved in the mosque activities, my academic status, and affiliation with the university positioned me as an outsider (Hill-Collins, 1990).

My hybrid and intersecting positionalities kept me at a critical distance from the girls' stories (Sandoval, 2000) that enabled me to see "patterns that may be more difficult for those immersed in the situation to see" (Hill-Collins, 2004, p. 104). This location or status of outsider-within is what bell hooks (2004) calls the "space of my theorizing" (p. 154), the location in which I confronted the silences on the *hijab* discourse and came to insights about my body stories and the girl's too.

The Secondary Participants

As the study proceeded, I was in constant contact with the parents of Layla, Dojua, Abby, and Amy. Almost every week I was arranging for the girls' pickup on Saturdays and/or discussing and getting the parents' approval for a change of plan or activity. I met with the parents at their work places and homes, at the restaurant of Dojua's father, and at the university activity center. The process of initiating and maintaining the relationships with all the girls' parents in this study was crucial in maintaining entry throughout the study (Hamzeh & Oliver, 2010). Building relationships with the parents was a challenging process that took a great deal of time and communication. Also, it was a process directly shaped by balancing the differences of our *muslimness*.

In the following stories in relation to each parent, I demonstrate the junctions of initiating trust then solidifying and maintaining the relationship with all them as secondary participants in the study.

The Mothers

The mothers of Layla, Dojua, Abby, and Amy negotiated our differences on the appropriateness of the study's activities and paces at several crossings in the study. They exchanged information about their understanding of the study and my eligibility to enter their daughters' lives. They were the main contacts to first allow me in, then to introduce me to the fathers, the formal decision makers to gaining entry. However, throughout the study, the girls' mothers were more involved than the fathers in the details of the decision to give me permission every Saturday. At a certain point, the mothers declared me their ally and thus trusted me as an insider in their daughter's lives. As a result, they gave me access in what was a relatively conservative and protective Muslim community.

Malikah, Layla's mother, was a White American woman in her forties. At the time of the study, she worked as a transcriber at Amy's father's neurology clinic. She was the breadwinner of the family since Layla's father was a student at the time. Malikah converted to Islam after marrying Layla's father at the beginning of her thirties and after having three boys from a previous marriage. She was the first mother I met at the mosque early in the study.

Early in the pilot study, Malikah showed her trust in me one time when Layla did not show up to Sunday class. Malikah told me that her husband had grounded Layla home that day because she was asking, "to do too much" with her school friends. Malikah expressed her fear that her husband would send Layla to her grandmother's house in Saudi Arabia. At that moment, she said to me, "I cannot live without her, she is my only daughter." I was very sympathetic and I suggested an article to help the father understand how important it was for Muslim girls to get more involved in extracurricular activities. She was welcoming. I mailed her the article and since then, I felt we had a mutual interest, Layla's wellbeing, and the beginning of a trusting relationship. This incident created a bond between us that was evident in her role of organizing the mothers to meet my advisor, visit the activity center and secure it as the study's site. Later she also connected me with two other mothers when I needed more girls to join the study. With this, Malikah showed her support to the study and her understanding of its benefits to the girls. She also expressed her interest in having Layla learn swimming and doing something useful in her spare time.

Through the women's group in the mosque, Malikah was active in the local Muslim community. Early in the summer, she called me to join her in meeting a group of female university students researching the faith of Islam for a world religion course. With this request, she was drawing on the trust between us and on the common interest to counter increasingly racist perceptions of Muslims post-9/11. She introduced me as the "professor researching Muslim girls," and asked me to present to the guests my study and my interest in Muslim girls. She thought I should be able to portray the "positive" side of Muslims, as she said "isn't that what you are trying to do in your study too." This experience also helped me understand more of Malikah's world and her *muslimness* in relation to Layla's life. More importantly, it urged me become more flexible and more patient in negotiating any differences that would arise with the mothers throughout the study.

On other occasions, while Layla was getting ready in her room with the girls on Saturdays, I had the chance to chat with Malikah in the sitting room. Several times, Malikah would approve the activity of the day with this last minute chat. She was helping Layla expand her learning experiences and negotiate her father's strict conditions on her mobility and activities.

One Saturday, while waiting in the car with the girls outside Layla's house, Layla called me on my mobile excited to say that we can come down to finally meet her dad. After one second, she called back talking fast with a hyper but low voice and said, "just remember," and I interrupted her too quickly and said, "not to say or mention anything about you swimming without your headscarf?" She followed, "no, no, do not mention to him anything about our plans to go to Al Jisr last night." I said, "of course." In one second Samer, Layla's father, came out to greet me but at the same time, he apologized for leaving right away to get us doughnuts for breakfast. When he left, I went in the sitting room, the girls disappeared with Layla, and then her mother came in and greeted me. Malikah was by now aware that her daughter had attended a football game in *Al Jiser,* though Layla's father would never have approved. This incident marked another crucial event in solidifying the relationship with Layla's mother and in giving me a green light into Layla's time until the end of the study. Afterwards, I did not directly ask for permission from Malikah because she allowed Layla to independently coordinate her time meeting us on Saturdays until the end of the study.

Khatimah, Dojua's mother, was a 40-year-old Algerian-Arab who immigrated to the United States with her family 9 years ago. She had a bachelor degree from an Algerian university. She worked with her husband at their family restaurant-business, Marrakech. Khatimah wore a headscarf in public.

Not until I spent hours visiting her at her restaurant and talking about the "homeland" and living in "strangeness of the exile," the difficulties of immigrating and living in exile, bringing up children away from the bigger family or away from Algeria, her life in Algeria, and my work and my family in Jordan, did I feel she was more relaxed and somehow opening the gate to trust me in Dojua's life. After this, she told me often "I trust you and I trust leaving Dojua with you." Every time I picked Dojua up early in the morning to accompany me to Al Jiser, where Abby lived, Khatimah would stand at the door waving good-bye and pointing to her eyes with her index finger, meaning "protect my daughter with your eyes." In other words, she handed me the responsibility of protecting Dojua with utmost trust. Khatimah's trust in me was crucial in enabling Dojua to be the most independent among the girls and to assume the responsibility of coordinating our meetings even after the study was over.

Zeena, Abby's mother, was an Algerian-American in her mid-forties who immigrated to the United States with her family 10 years ago. She was one of the mothers I had the least contact with because she lived in Al Jiser. She worked as a dental hygienist though she was licensed as a dentist in Algeria. Zeena did not wear a headscarf in public.

Two months into the study, Abby reported that her mother was not supportive of her participation. She said, "She thinks we are playing around." Despite her initial impression of the study and the distance between the two cities—which decreased my chances to meet her directly—I decided to communicate with Zeena directly and more frequently. And thus, I made it a point when picking up Abby to make sure I spent a few minutes with Zeena to chat. I informed her of the good times we were having and the value and the benefit the experiences were bringing to the girls. I was also trying to bond with her as an educated *arabyyah-muslimah* my age living away from the "homeland."

With time, I felt Zeena was warmer, even though she still gave the impression that she was not so active in the decisions involving Abby's life. Her support to the study and her trust in me became apparent when I asked to meet Abby in December for one more time to do the member check. Without asking Abby's father, she quickly gave me the permission after a short chat on the phone.

Jamilah, Amy's mother, was a "Pakistani-Punjabi-American" in her mid-forties who immigrated to the United States with her family 11 years ago. Jamilah had a bachelor degree in political science from a university in Pakistan and was a homemaker. In public, Jamilah wore a loose and light cloth kind of headscarf that usually matched her Pakistani "traditional" clothes.

Right from the beginning, Jamilah was very encouraging and welcoming to include Amy in the study especially due to its physical activity component. Jamilah made it clear that she was fully in charge of Amy's daily activities and that her studies were a priority. She also informed me that she shared with Amy's father, Ali, the decisions about Amy's life. This meant I did not have to go through him for permissions. Jamilah signed the consent form herself as I read it to her the first day she dropped Amy off at the activity center.

Right from the beginning, Jamilah was showing me her appreciation of how much Amy was enjoying her time in the activities of this project. This meant that Amy shared with her what we were doing weekly. Additionally, I took the opportunity to always stop and talk to Jamilah at the door when I brought Amy home. I shared with her generalities about some of what I learned spending time with the girls. Often, she expressed her acknowledgment of the value of the study and asked very few questions. Mainly we were both bonding and in agreement on the fact that the girls were having fun in health related activities and that they were building good friendships with each other.

She invited me more than once to eat over but I only accepted small visits after the long hours with the girls. I tasted her food a couple of times as a gesture to strengthen our bond, learning that when one is offered food in her house it is an insult to refuse it. Food was also a subject to talk about with Jamilah since I was concerned about the girls' style of eating. Jamilah was very happy for this connection and for encouraging good eating habits with her daughter. This was also a confirmation of her trust in me and in my literacies, that is, I understood the difference between halal food, permissible to Muslim, and junk and fast food. She said more than once as she praised Amy for eating mostly her home cooking, "Eating halal and home cooking is better for Amy's health than the bad American fast food."

Throughout the study, I tried to meet the mothers directly when possible as well as to learn about their roles in their daughters' lives through the girls themselves. I did this in order to keep the door open with them as long as possible and to find ways to encourage the girls to keep communicating with their mothers on issues they confided in me. Often the girls expressed that they were confused and frustrated about their fathers' restricting decisions and that their mothers were more often complicit with such decisions. Abby said, "I don't tell her [her mother] anything about what I feel … I do but like I don't tell her all that we talk about." Such comments from the girls concerned me that the girls were under-communicating or miscommunicating with their parents and going into some sort of isolating silences. Therefore, often I entered conversations with Malikah, Khatimah, and Jamilah, the mothers in town, about the girls concerns but without disclosing specifics the girls told me about or violating the girls' confidentiality. It was a way to strengthen my alliance with the mothers and at the same time support the girls' attempts to make sense of their experiences.

The Fathers

In this study, I had to negotiate a brief but very crucial relationship with three of the four fathers. Nonetheless, I was only able to enter the men's domains because first I passed the scrutiny of the mothers and second because they arranged the meetings with their husbands. However, even with the mothers' permission, I still had to prove my legitimacy and dependability with each one of the three fathers differently. That is, though the mother's approval was necessary for the official permission and the signature of the consent forms, I still had to earn the father's trust and respect in order to maintain a longer entry.

To make this gain, I used my insider's most important asset, speaking Arabic with each one of them. On the one hand, my Jordanian-Arabic was very close to Layla's father's Saudi accent, which helped me communicate easily with him. Yet, on the other hand, with Dojua and Abby's fathers, I had to make an effort and modify my accent towards classical Arabic in order to accommodate their Algerian-Arabic and be as intelligible as possible. All three fathers were more comfortable speaking Arabic than English. Therefore, my effort in speaking Arabic was well received.

Additionally, meeting the three fathers in their "man world" I was first an outsider. But once I took the time to discuss the colonizing history of the French to their countries of origin, and to ponder over current political events in the Arab and Muslim regions, I began to gain their trust. Speaking Arabic and discussing history and politics were necessary tactics to make the entry to the study as an insider. The following stories reveal how each of the fathers gave me his explicit permission by signing the consent form. But more importantly, these stories show how their *manly* words expressed their implicit trust in my work with their daughters and granted me access throughout the study period.

Samer, Layla's father, was a Saudi-Arabian man in his early forties. Samer was a student of computer science at the local community college. Samer was the hardest father to get to meet. I had worked with his daughter in the first stage of the study but never had the chance to meet him. At the beginning of the summer of 2006, I tried to make an appointment with him directly but he was either sleeping or very busy studying. Thus, meeting him was not possible without Dojua's father lobbying and certainly not without the approval from Malikah, his wife. Nonetheless, I had to wait for the appropriate opportunity to be invited to his house by Layla and her mother.

Every time I had the chance to drop Layla at home, I would ask her if her father was available to meet. One Saturday morning when it was pouring rain in Al Hilal and after I was back from the full round picking up three of the girls between the two cities, we arrived at the last stop, Layla's house. Layla popped out and waved inviting us in. It was already 1 P.M.—usually we started at 11 A.M.—but I knew by then that we were not going to do any swimming, so I took this invitation without hesitation and went in with the girls.

Samer was so proud to invite me in his house. He said, "Finally I meet you and finally you give me the honor to come to my home." Samer's welcoming attitude reflected a prominent trait in *badawi* (person born in a nomadic tribe) hospitality. It is a reflection of a *badawi*'s sheer generosity expressed once a guest walks into his/her territory. This familiar trait put me immediately at ease after a long awaited period of estrangement before meeting Samer. Moreover, Samer called me "cousin" once he realized I was born in a Jordanian tribe. He wanted to think that my tribe was connected to his big tribe from the northeast borders of Saudi, which is also on the Jordanian southern borders. Samer's emphasis on the tribal bonding between us was his way to implicitly show his approval of my authenticity as an insider. This gave him another reason to grant me trust and respect. To illustrate further and contextualize my meeting with Samer, I share what I wrote my advisor that day in the following story.

Samer, Layla's father, strikes me as a very generous and kind person, but certainly and not surprisingly very authoritative. We talked about all sorts of issues—politics, America, living here, protecting females in this Western society etc. Of course, we spoke in Arabic while nobody in the room including the brothers and the mother understood what we were saying. I already knew a good rapport was building with Samer so I endured much of his preaching monologue as he presented his racist and sexist opinions and his fixed perspectives of how all Arabs and Muslims are or should be especially with "their" women. I listened much more than I talked. He dug my roots and origins in Jordan and he thought his father knows my grandfather who was the first medical doctor in Jordan and who treated the poor for no fees. After an hour or more, and once he made a tribal and familial connection, he sort of gave me legitimacy and a pass to enter. He did not ask one thing about why and what we are doing in this group or this project. I tried shortly to describe the points in the consent form but since he wanted to show me his trust, he said that there is no need to go through this and signed the consent form. He said while laughing, "Cousin, there are no formalities between us from now on you can do whatever you want with my girl." Yes, I think I got his approval for being enough of an insider to trust.

Iyad, Dojua's father, was an Algerian-Arab man in his late forties. Iyad had a bachelor degree from an Algerian university. With his wife, he owned and ran the family's restaurant-business, Marrakech. Iyad played a pivotal role with the men in this study. He was the easiest among the fathers to initiate a relationship with. He was also the only father I continued to visit, and thus, I maintained a growing and strong friendship to this day.

Early June, the day I met Dojua, I met Iyad in his restaurant, Marrakech. He was very welcoming and receptive from the minute I said,

"Salam." A few days later, when Iyad's wife informed me that her husband should sign the consent form, I immediately arranged to meet him at the restaurant. When I walked in, he was sitting with his cousin who had just arrived from Algeria, and they were chatting while there were no clients around. He offered me coffee and introduced me to his cousin, then said, "the minute I met Manal, I don't know how but she entered my heart." He repeated this statement again, once when he introduced me to Ghazi, his Algerian friend, Abby's father; and other times when I went to eat with friends at his restaurant.

The day I presented the consent form to Iyad, I asked him if he preferred that I review the clauses of the consent form in Arabic. I knew he was not comfortable with written English. He pushed the forms aside while laughing. Dismissing the need to read the form, he said, "This is an absurd request to ask a brother, this is too American." In this move, Iyad was expressing that I was already an insider and that he trusted me enough not to read the content of the form in order to sign it. This was Iyad's way to show his awareness of my authenticity as an insider and to show his kind of trust in me. Once Iyad signed the consent form he openly signaled the beginning of my relationship with him, and consequentially allowed me entry to Dojua's life.

Afterwards, I continued to visit him any time in Marrakech to have political chats and frequently to eat there with friends and colleagues. He would call me often to check on me and to see if I needed anything around Muslim holidays. I would see him every Saturday as I dropped off Dojua at the restaurant before her weekend shift helping her mother that night. He knew I was supportive of his business and I knew he was supportive of my study. A few times, he said he wanted to have a party for me when I graduate.

Iyad's friendliness and support were consistent and strong even at junctions when he was covertly examining my insiderness. His spontaneous trust in me opened the door for a friendship that proved to be very important to sustaining entry into the girls' lives but also one that took much time, care, and cultivation.

Ghazi, Abby's father was an Algerian-American in his mid-fifties. Ghazi has a science graduate degree from an Algerian university. He worked as a science curriculum consultant to the school district of Al Jiser. Ghazi, an Algerian-Arab in his mid-fifties, is my roommate's colleague, and through her, I first connected with him. A few times at the beginning of the summer, we talked on the phone and I introduced the study to him. He expressed that he was generally supportive of the study and Abby's participation. However, at the end of July, Ghazi and Zeena still seemed hesitant about their commitment to the study. I asked Iyad for help. He immediately called Ghazi and invited him to visit. The next weekend both

Ghazi and Zeena drove to Al Hilal from Al Jiser (an hour ride) in response to Iyad's invitation. They visited him at his restaurant, Marrakech; while Abby spent time with us. Later that day, I met Ghazi and his wife as they waited for Abby at Marrakech. It was the first time we met. We had an important conversation that initiated the trust and respect needed to start.

When I first walked into the restaurant, Ghazi stood to greet me. I shook hands with him without hesitation because I made the assumption since Zeena was without a headscarf, that they were not so conservative. That is, I would not break a modesty rule if I extended my hand to shake his hand. As I stood next to the table and I was still thanking them both for giving me permission to spend time with Abby, Ghazi abruptly gestured and led me to the furthest side spot in the restaurant. For a good 10 minutes, we stood there talking while all the girls sat at one table across the room glancing at us.

In the conversation above, Ghazi started being diplomatic but when I began explaining how crucial this time is for the girls and that as an educator I am learning a lot about their worlds, he began to listen. Soon after, he seemed to agree that the girls would benefit by spending the time in the study with me. However, this meant to him that I would be able to "correct them because they are confused between two opposite cultures, being Muslim and living in the Western American society." I continued trying to explain to him that "correcting" the girls is not the aim of the study, his assumption about their cultural confusion is not mine, and choosing one of "the cultures" is not my aim either. I explained further that my role is not to help them offset the process of "Americanization" or to help them "preserve their *Islamness*" as he put it. Nonetheless, he continued, "It is a huge responsibility on me as a father to protect her here [in the United States]." He was again assuming I was going to help him "protect" his daughter from some bad influence she is exposed to in the United States. I could not get it through to him that part of my role was to invite the girls to become critical of their context and eventually to be more independent in their living a healthy and successful life regardless of their geographical location or faith. This conversation was a struggle for me as I tried to balance explaining to Ghazi the study's aims with what he assumed is *the* way to instruct Muslim girls living in the West. I was not sure he was going to approve Abby's participation in the study's activities.

However, I tried to persist and continue the conversation with Ghazi on political current events in the Algeria. Later he asked, "Do you know about the Algerian history with the French?" I answered enthusiastically, "of course," as I knew this was an opportunity to find something in common between us and open a chance to negotiate our differences on "how Muslim girls should be instructed." He was trying to explain his point of view that protecting Abby or women in the Muslim culture is a must and "it is the responsibility of the man, the head of the family." He was very confident that I agreed with his view since I was a Muslim and an Arab. He went on to explain further,

> Alhmdulilah [thank Allah] the Algerians were able to resist the French colonizers unlike the submissive Tunisians who became French (Western or non-Muslim) in dealing with their women ... you know the French broke the Tunisian family by giving freedom to women but they could not do it with the Algerians.

Ghazi was beaming with pride emphasizing how Muslim the Algerians are. He expressed that this was due to their ability to resist the colonizers by controlling their women's bodies. He added to emphasize his point about the strength of his *muslimness* as an Algerian, "You see I only send Abby to houses of Muslim families and now there are none close to our house." At this point of the conversation, I began to feel that Ghazi was expressing to me his disapproval of the study and thus my chances to work with Abby were diminishing. I was struggling to find a way with Ghazi in order to gain his trust whether by bringing up any aspects of my insiderness or my educational intentions in this study. However, once Ghazi was explaining how women need to be protected and how good Muslims are compared to Americans, I abruptly shifted the conversation to more common grounds.

I shared with him one of my goals for the study was to present to the girls postcolonial Algerian literary works I am familiar with. This was my way of drawing them to their parents' background and history. Once I listed names of authors and books, Ghazi was elated and expressed that he was happy to have Abby work with somebody like me to learn more about his "beloved homeland." This part of our conversation seemed to bring Ghazi's awareness to my authenticity as an insider and respect me enough to sign the consent form that day. After this encounter and once I took responsibility for Abby's transportation from and to Al Jiser, I did minimal work to maintain a good relationship with Ghazi that assured Abby's participation in the study.

During this conversation, a couple of times I looked over to Abby and I think I saw fearful questioning in her eyes. She was not sure I was going to gain her father's trust and be able to keep her in the group. Well, later I talked to her with the girls and only conveyed the positive responses of her father and his approval to this project and her participation in it. She responded expressing disbelief "really!"

The informed consent forms signed by the four girls were different from those signed by their parents (Appendixes A and B). In the approval by the university's institutional review board, it is specified that data from

the girls could only be disclosed to the parents with the girls' explicit consent. This condition for releasing data was designed to ensure the anonymity and confidentiality of the girls. I highlighted and discussed the
designated paragraph describing this process with every parent and girl,
each of whom then signed a consent form.

Additionally, I obtained a letter of permission to work within the
women's quarters of the local mosque from the all-male board of trustees
(Appendix C). The head of the Department of Physical Education, Recreation and Dance was supportive of the study. He gave me permission to
work with the girls at the activity center, the home of the Department of
Physical Education, Recreation and Dance.

At the end of the study, I sent each parent a thank you letter to express
my appreciation and make a closure to this stage in our relationship.
Dojua's father called me and thanked me for my time and effort and
asked me to stay in touch and to keep dropping by his restaurant anytime.
Five years after the start of the study, I am still in contact with Dojua and
her parents and Amy and her mother.

DATA COLLECTION AND ANALYSIS

I collected data for this study in two stages over a period of 14 months.
Phase 1 was a pilot study that lasted from October 2005 to April 2006.
Phase 2 was the formal study, which lasted from June 2006 to December
2006. In the first 7 months, I met with the girls 10 times for approximately 2 hours each time at the women's quarters of the local mosque.
During the second 7 months, I met with the four girls 17 times for
approximately 9–11 hours each time. Mainly, the activities for this study
took place in, (1) the gym, pool, study room, and exercise rooms of a university activity center; and (2) other public places in town—the mall,
cafés, et cetera. Independently, the girls selected and/or suggested the
study's activities and places.

In order to understand how the girls experienced their bodies, I used a
variety of interactive data collection methods used by critical feminist
researchers working with young people. These methods included, (1) filling out a self-mapping questionnaire, "Help me Know you Better"
(Appendix D), that sketched some basic information about each girls'
intersections of her identity, family members', school interests, place and
activities of interest, and the ways they saw themselves as Muslims (Sirin &
Fine, 2008); (2) asking the girls to take photos of events, places, and people
in their lives that they wanted to share with me or with the other girls—I
provided them with disposable cameras but they also brought in previously
taken photos (Oliver & Lalik, 2000); (3) selecting and cutting images from
fashion and music magazines of their choice (Oliver, 2003); (4) asking the

girls to do free-writing in their journals with prompts like "I am …," "What if …," and "What kind of fun gets you in trouble?" (Oliver & Lalik, 2000); (5) exchanging e-mails between the girls and I in which they elaborated on some issues they were questioning at the time; (6) creating a body collage and individual scrapbooks to represent and describe themselves to my advisor in an oral presentation (Appendixes E and F); and (7) engaging in small group conversations. All conversations were audio recorded and field notes were taken after each session with the girls.

Creating a body collage and individual scrapbooks were methods that emerged as suggestions from the girls themselves and developed out of our conversations and dialogues around how they or I would directly answer the basic question of this study to a general audience—if we had to. That is, what are the tools, language, and media that would help them and me express and represent their lived experiences to an outsider. Specifically, they felt there was a need to explain to their peers in school who they are as Muslims. Though, taking photos and cutting images from magazines was a method I planned to use in the design of the study to open the girls to express more about their lives, they decided to use their photos and images to make a body collage and scrapbooks too. The girls suggested inviting my advisor, as an outsider, and presenting to her their stories through these two productions.

I used the girls' journals to open a private space for conversations with each one of them. This activity also inspired some of them to write me more through private and group e-mails that continued to flow to my inbox many months after the project was officially over.

All of the individual small or big group conversations I had with the girls and sometimes with their parents were like "dialogical interviews" (Thomas, 2005, p. 246). In every encounter I had with the girls or their parents, I listened carefully and followed up with questions or comments at the time of the conversation. I also made mental notes that I tried to put down in my field notes in order to initiate a deeper dialogue in the next meeting. Particularly, as we moved in these conversations, we listened more to each other and came up with more questions, and thus, co-created meaning as went along (Hesse-Biber & Leavy, 2007).

Data sources included: (1) 4 self-mapping questionnaires; (2) 17 task sheets from work sessions with the girls; (3) 17 transcripts of audio recordings of group meetings in the study room (22 hours); (4) 35 e-mails Manal exchanged with the girls; (5) 35 pages of private journal entries by the girls; (6) over 300 digital photos that Manal or the girls took; (7) a poster of a body collage and individual scrapbooks the girls created; (8) lists of the words and quotes pasted on the collage and scrapbooks; (9) 15 audio recordings of informal conversations in the car, cafés, etc. (18 hours); and

(10) 210 pages of field notes, my reflection memos, and e-mails exchanged with my advisor.

Data analysis was threefold. First, I transcribed each audio recording after meeting with the girls. I read the transcripts while simultaneously listening to the audio recording. "Memoing and coding" (Hesse-Biber & Leavy 2007, p. 332) were two ways by which I identified repeated words and concepts. In coding, I literally read every line in the transcribed data then took segments directly from the repeated text and gave them theme names (Hesse-Biber & Leavy, 2007). Simultaneously in memoing, I wrote my notes and impressions, which elevated the literal codes to descriptive categories or sub-themes (Hesse-Biber & Leavy, 2007). In this layer of analysis, I was making meaning of the data and grouping my memos to inform the purpose of the project. I was also looking for themes that took the project in directions I had not anticipated.

Second, I compiled all textual data sources into one document then sorted them out in piles according to themes and the sub-themes that began to emerge in the step one. At this point, I began to do an elaborate thematical analysis, or what Hesse-Biber and Leavy (2007) call "focused coding" (p. 333). In other words, I began to deveil and (re)read the different emergent *hijabs* stories of Layla, Dojua, Abby, and Amy. Next, I compared all of the emerging descriptive categories or sub-themes in every theme in different data sources in order to inform the purpose of this study (Denzin & Lincoln, 2005). Third, I rewrote the thematic groups into vignettes, which accordingly created the theoretical interpretations and the claims of this study (Denzin & Lincoln, 2005).

INSIDER'S METHODS AND CRITICAL SELF-REFLEXIVITY

In this section, I discuss two major feminist critical methods that also framed the *deveiling* methodology, (1) classical Islamic insider's methods and (2) critical self-reflexivity. These two *deveiling* methods weaved in negotiating the spatial and relational contexts of the study and in making the analysis of the data and more specifically as I discuss below.

One, relying on the conceptualization in Chapter 2, Mernissi's (1991) use of the classical Islamic insider's methods such as *asbab al nuzul* to decontextualize the Qur'anic text and *isnad* and *matn* to (de)authenticate the misogynistic *ahadīth*, was helpful throughout the study. Mernissi's (1991) use of insider's classical Islamic interpretive tools and the resulting deconstruction of the *hijabs* helped identify the emerging themes in gaining access in the study (Chapter 4) and in the girls' physical activities stories (Chapter 5). More importantly, Mernissi's (1991) use of insider's methods and the *deveiling* of a gendering discourse, helped identify the

possibilities the girls opened to go beyond the popular fixed representations of the physical *hijabs*. It exposed the multiple meanings of these *muslim* girls' experiences with the three *hijabs*—visual, spatial, and ethical—
and the possibilities of seeing beyond or crossing the fourth *hijab*—spiritual (Chapter 5). This was a process of *deveiling* the taken-for-granted in
the lives of these four *muslim* girls. Mernissi's work with the insider's
methods, as *deveiling* methods, showed me as researcher how a *muslim*
may stay away from being blinded from deeper knowledge as he/she
"does not know how to explore his [her] extraordinary capacities for multiple perceptions" (Mernissi, 1991, p. 95). That is, Mernissi's deconstruction of the *hijabs* as a gendering discourse helped in understanding the
complexity of the lives of *muslim* girls in this study and sparked my imagination of *deveiling* pedagogies.

Two, drawing heavily on critical feminist research scholars especially
Hesse-Biber and Leavy (2007) and their conceptualization of critical self-
reflexivity or "strong reflexivity ... [as] the manifestation of strong objectivity through method" (p. 15), I was able to negotiate my relationships
with the parents from the start of the study, but especially negotiate my
differences with them on the *hijabs* (Chapter 4). As the main researcher in
this study and an Arab-Mulsim critical feminist, I used critical self-reflexivity as,

> the process through which a researcher recognizes, examines, and under-
> stands how his or her own social background and assumptions can intervene
> in the research process.... To practice reflexivity means to acknowledge that
> all knowledge is affected by the social conditions under which it is produced
> and that it is grounded in both the social location and the social biography
> of the observer and the observed. (Hesse-Biber & Leavy, 2007, p. 129)

That is, I practiced critical self-reflexivity by drawing on my insider/
inbetweener positionalities "as both a hindrance and a resource toward
achieving knowledge throughout the research process" (Hesse-Biber &
Leavy 2007, p. 15). I used critical self-reflexivity with my insider's literacies of Arabic, Islam, *muslims*, and the *hijabs*, to stay cognizant of my own
standpoints towards the *hijabs*, and thus, stay more open to negotiate my
differences on the *hijabs'* interpretations *among/with* the four *muslim* girls
themselves and their parents too. Weekly debriefings of face-to-face meetings and detailed e-mails with my advisor, an outsider with a long experience in working with girls and activist research, helped me stay reflexive
about mediating my difference with the parents. These debriefings represented the many "reflexivity samplings" of this study (Hesse-Biber &
Piatelli, 2007, p. 496). These samplings included my perspectives right
after meeting the girls every week in which I expressed what I learned,
what I was questioning and/or what I was concerned about. They also

included my reflections on how I was initially negotiating my differences with the parents over the *hijabs*. My practice of critical self-reflexivity was a major methodological tool with which I became aware of my constantly shifting standpoints towards the *hijabs*, and thus, more attentive to the *hijab*'s multiple subtleties in the lives of the four Muslim girls (Chapter 5). Critical and strong self-reflexivity enabled me to continually examine my positionalities and make visible the silences in the data. It enabled me to notice and interpret the silences, and eventually, access an alternative knowledge or insights on how the girls' different ways of negotiating the *hijabs* created the possibilities of change throughout the study (Fine, 1994; Hesse-Biber & Piatelli, 2007). Particularly, maintaining critical self-reflexivity allowed me to persevere during the uncertainty of the entry process and to negotiate the long access process to the girls' lives (Hamzeh & Oliver, 2010).

SUMMARY

In this chapter, I mapped out the feminist *deveiling* methodology that guided the study. I , an *arabyyah-muslimah*, worked with four Muslim girls seeking to understand how they negotiated the *hijab* discourse in the two southwestern U.S. border towns of Al Hilal and Al Jiser. This was a collaborative project in which I used classical Islamic insider's methods and critical self-reflexivity. These two *deveiling* methods helped me in negotiating the spatial contexts and relationships in the study; and consequently interpreting the data.

What follows are the main stories of this study about *deveiling* access to the girls lives and about *deveiling* the *hijabs*.

CHAPTER 4

DEVEILING RESEARCH ACCESS

What do you mean by wanting to understand how our girls experience their bodies ... we cannot allow you to conduct your research in the mosque unless you guarantee that you will not be talking about sex or sexual behavior with the girls. (The head of the local mosque council)

In the previous chapter, I discussed how negotiating the location and relationships of the project was key to gaining access. In this chapter, I analyze in more detail the process of gaining research access into the lives of Layla, Dojua, Abby, and Amy, the four Muslim girls in this study, which became pivotal to the start and continuation of this research project. Specifically, I identify four challenges that emerged in the process of gaining and sustaining access throughout the study duration and they included, (1) being Muslim enough, (2) *inshallah* (Allah or God willing), (3) being modest enough, and (4) *haram* (forbidden). The four challenges were markers of difference on both *muslimness* and the interpretations of the *hijabs* and the *hijab* discourse between the girls, the parents, and myself.

BEING MUSLIM ENOUGH

There are five pillars to Islam: (1) faith or belief in the Oneness of God, Allah, and the finality of the prophethood of Mohammed; (2) establishment of the five daily prayers; (3) self-purification through fasting during the month of Ramadan; (4) charity by giving to the needy; and (5) the

Pedagogies of Deveiling: Muslim Girls and the Hijab Discourse,
pp. 75–86

pilgrimage to Mecca for those who are able. The private or public practices of theses pillars are some of the main signifiers of the "scope" of one's *muslimness*.

My *muslimness* or being Muslim enough emerged as the first difference with the parents, and thus, the challenge to my eligibility to gain entry. Given that it is mostly taken-for-granted that anyone who is born in a Muslim family is automatically a believer in the first pillar of Islam, thus, with my Muslim name, the first pillar did not emerge as a marker of difference over my *muslimness*. From the first day of the study when I met most of the adults for the first time, I spoke Arabic as I introduced myself, "I am Manal Hamzeh[1] from Jordan. I am a doctoral student in the local university ... I am interested in learning about Muslim girls in this town." My Muslim name, my country of birth, Jordan,[2] my use of Arabic as my *home* language, and my interest to work with Muslims girls in this study, may have reflected my *muslimness* in the subtlety of the first pillar of Islam. That is, I was Muslim enough and allowed to start communicating about the study.

However, the difference over my *muslimness* emerged also, in relation to how much I observed the second and the third pillars of Islam. The degree of my adherence to these pillars determined how much of an insider I was, and thus whether I was Muslim enough to be trusted with the girls. Though I did not directly have to negotiate my *muslimness* by practicing the five daily prayers, the second pillar of Islam, it did subtly seep in as a marker of difference with the parents and challenged my gaining entry. At the beginning of the pilot study, I was very conscious of the fact that being present in a mosque for long hours would present a higher possibility for a prayer call by the *mu'athin*.[3] Usually, I went to meet the girls at the mosque between 12 and 4 P.M.—the time that coincided with the *dhuhr* (noon) and/or *'asr* (afternoon) prayers. I feared getting invited to join the women for a group prayer, thus obliged to pray. While I do not practice the five daily prayers, I am generally knowledgeable of the rituals associated with this pillar. However, at this point, I did not want to pretend that I observe this pillar and just go through the rituals or be obliged to decline the invitation by revealing that I was a *Muslimah* who does not do the five daily prayers. Taking any of those two options may have been read that I was not Muslim enough. In other words, had I been obliged to do any of the daily prayers in the mosque with the women might have revealed my nonobservance of this pillar altogether, and thus, might have jeopardized the possibility of gaining entry right from the beginning.

During the holy month of Ramadan, which overlapped with the last month of this study, I also had to negotiate and maintain entry in response to fasting the whole month, the third pillar of Islam. Again, the girls' parents assumed that I followed the usual rituals and religious demands of Ramadan. On a couple of occasions, they invited me into their community for *ifttar*,[4] the main meal of the day in which they break their fasting at sunset. Given that I did not practice the rituals of Ramadan, I was once more at risk of facing the parents' judgment for not being Muslim enough. On the second day of Ramadan, I was visiting Dojua's father, at his restaurant. As we began comparing Ramadan food between Algeria and Jordan, suddenly he asked me, "Do you pray every day at home and fast Ramadan?" I felt trapped so I said, "No, I do not pray five times a day." I tried to negotiate this direct scrutiny on being Muslim enough by immediately elaborating, "I interpret Islam differently and faith is a private matter in my life." Dojua's father argued that there is only one way of interpreting the pillars of Islam. However, right away he asked me to join his wife and the other women for the special evening Ramadan prayers at the mosque. His insistence to bring me closer to his way of perceiving and practicing Islam made me feel more uncomfortable and fearful of losing entry. If I continued to argue or tried to excuse myself from his request, I would be revealing more of how I did not pray daily, did not pursue Ramadan evening group prayers after *ifttar*, and did not fast during Ramadan. I feared Dojua's father would decide that I was not Muslim enough to work with his daughter and pull me out in the middle of the study. Given the closeness of the local Muslim community, such an incident would surely jeopardize my access to the other girls as well.

In hopes of negotiating my way out, I explained that I had a nonreligious upbringing and that I never entered a mosque except in Jerusalem and only out of my interest in Islamic history and architecture. At this point, Dojua's father gently rescinded his request but insisted upon inviting me for *ifttar* with his family every sundown at his restaurant or at his home. Rather than declining his gracious invitation the first time, I used night classes as an excuse for not being able to join them and politely asked for a rain check. I hoped that I might have left Dojua's father thinking I was observing Ramadan's rituals of fasting but in my own privacy or I was Muslim enough regardless. However, one Saturday, before the end Ramadan, coming into the restaurant with all the girls, I accepted the invitation of Dojua's mother at the end of her shift for an *ifttar* meal. Dojua's father joined us later to have desert having had his *ifttar* at the mosque with men and after the special prayers as a group. At that point, at least particularly to Dojua's parents, I qualified as Muslim enough in relation to fasting in Ramadan, thus maintaining my entry and ability to continue working with Dojua and the other girls.

INSHALLAH

Muslims commonly and frequently use the Arabic term *inshallah*, which means in Arabic, God willing. *Inshallah* is a central principle in the Muslim's faith of obedience to One God, Allah,

وَلا تَقُولَنَّ لِشَيْءٍ إِنِّي فَاعِلٌ ذَلِكَ غَدًا. إِلاَّ أَن يَشَاء اللَّهُ وَاذْكُر رَّبَّكَ إِذَا نَسِيتَ وَقُلْ عَسَى أَن يَهْدِيَنِ رَبِّي لِأَقْرَبَ مِنْ هَذَا رَشَدًا.

(القرآن الكريم، ٢٣:١٨، ٢٤)

And do not say of anything: Surely I will do it tomorrow. Except if Allah will. And remember thy Lord when thou forgettest, and say: It may be that my Lord guideth me unto a nearer way of truth than this. (The Qur'an, 18:23, 18:24)

As such, *inshallah* means the Muslim's peaceful submission to Allah's will. In other words, when a Muslim utters the word *inshallah* he/she submits to Allah, and therefore he/she is confirmed as a Muslim. That is, *inshallah* means that life events are not in the hands of the Muslim but rather are in God's hands—dependent on Allah's will. Practically, this implies that a Muslim may not confirm plans and will deal with them as uncertainties until they actually happen. In the context of this study, the utterance *inshallah* emerged as the second challenge to my eligibility to gain entry. Every time the parents uttered "*inshallah*," they made a vague commitment to the continuation of the study. This persistent tentative commitment meant that the study was always provisional.

At the beginning of the study after having explained the consent forms to the mothers and the girls, they all took copies home to get their fathers' signatures. Several times, I had to call and remind the girls' mothers to return the signed consent form. They would say to me "*inshallah* next time." In this instant, *inshallah* kept the access for the first planned meeting very unsure. It took meeting with the fathers on three different occasions and locations to get their signatures on the consent forms.

As the study moved on, *inshallah* was prominent every time I dropped the girls at home. Each Saturday, I would stop to greet the mothers and to tell them what the plan was for the next week. When I said, "I will pick them up next week" the mothers automatically would respond "*inshallah*." This response did not mean the girls would automatically join the next meeting. A couple of hours before every Saturday meeting, I had to place several calls to the mothers to assure the girls' attendance and thus, guarantee continual entry.

My linguistic/cultural literacies of Arabic and Islam allowed me to recognize that the parents' use of *inshallah* merely reflected their submission to the will of Allah, and not necessarily their unwillingness to have me continue working with the girls. Such literacy kept me open to accept the resulting uncertainty and to know better than rushing the parents for a commitment that they were not comfortable making. I was able to respond with patience and sometimes with repeated calls for clarifications, until the parents actually gave me permission for an activity or to plan with the girls.

BEING MODEST ENOUGH

Given that *al hishma*, modesty, is derived from the Arabic root *hshm*, to anger and to cause embarrassment (*Lisan Al Arab*), it is the virtue by which a Muslim maintains her/his moderation, humility, and respect (Mernissi, 1991). That is, Muslims must express their modesty by behaving respectfully in their lives especially by staying away from the forbiddens (El Guindi, 1999). Though modesty as such applies to men and women, this virtue has become more associated with Muslim women wearing a headscarf and not socializing with men in public. Arguably, modesty in dress and mobility in public has become a normalizing outcome of the dominant discourse which disciplined Muslim women's lives and gauges their submission to Islam (Badran, 1985). That is, Muslim women must practice modesty abiding by the three *hijabs* that I have discussed in Chapter 2. First the visual *hijab*, covering parts or all their bodies; second the spatial *hijab*, secluding them to private spaces away from public life; and third the ethical *hijab*, protecting them from forbidden behavior (Mernissi, 1991).

Wearing a headscarf is one of the most explicit visual representations of modesty implied by the *hijab* discourse on Muslim women's bodies in public (Ahmed, 1992). A headscarf like any other imposed visual *hijab*, is supposed to protect a Muslim female's body from a male gaze and hide her body to prevent men from being seduced by her sexual potential. The more subtle visual and spatial *hijabs* that oblige a Muslim woman to practice modesty are those that are inscribed on her behavior in public spaces. These are, (1) lowering her gaze in a man's presence; (2) restraining from shaking hands with men; (3) restraining from having any physical contact with any man outside her direct family; and (4) working and socializing in gender segregated public and private domains (Badran, 1995).

Being modest enough—observing the visual *hijab*—emerged as the third difference between the parents and myself and challenged my eligibility to gain entry. Modesty became another marker of difference that I had to negotiate between the participants and myself. In this study, the mothers adhered to a variety of practices and representations of modesty in dress. Two of the mothers wore a tight headscarf, one wore a loose thin scarf showing a lot of hair, and one did not wear a headscarf. Their practice of modesty in public spaces also varied. Three of the mothers worked in nonsegregated gendered public jobs while one worked in the privacy of her home. However, outside of work, all four mothers lived gender segregated social lives. That is, they did not socialize with men unless their husbands were present. When they attended functions at the mosque only when secluded from men in women designated quarters. In contrast, I never wore a headscarf and never lived a gender segregated social or public/professional life whether when I lived Jordan or other locations.

Throughout the study, I was aware of how I dressed and how I demonstrated my modesty in public while interacting with the girls' parents, especially with their fathers. For the parents to perceive me being modest enough I had to walk a fine line to balance what my modesty weighed in moral standing with what my cultural knowledge weighed in respectability. That is, if I sensed that the extent of my modesty in dress or behavior was not enough, I had to counter it with something of value to the parents, such as my ability to speak Arabic, to recite verbatim Qur'anic verses, or to reiterate Mohammed's teachings when an opportunity arose. The following are a few stories that illustrate how being modest enough challenged my access to the lives of the girls continually.

From the first moment of meeting the mothers and the female teachers in the mosque early in the pilot study, to meeting two of the fathers in their homes and one in his restaurant, I was anxiously and conscious of how "unveiled" I looked. That is, every time I was planning to meet the parents and the girls, I was cognizant of how I dressed differently from the mothers, not only by not wearing a headscarf, but also wearing what may reveal my legs, arms, shoulders, and chest or may somehow be a bit tight around my hips. My concerns stemmed from whether the parents would consider my modesty enough and thus, would allow me to enter their daughters' lives.

Before going into the mosque for the first time, I was apprehensive about having to put on at least a loose headscarf. In order to gain initial entry, I wanted to show my acknowledgment to the mothers' way of modesty in dress. Considering that the first day I met the girls and their mothers in the women's quarter of Al Hilal mosque, where all the women had taken off their headscarves; I was still very aware of myself going in without a headscarf. From then on when encountering the girls' parents, I consistently and intentionally wore clothes that were loose fitting and covered my upper arms and chest.

My willingness to embody a degree of the visual *hijab* was one way I tried to balance my modesty in dress with that of the mothers and teachers. In this, I thought I eased the tension of this difference between us and accordingly was hoping that they would grant me permission to work with their daughters. In other words, by not wearing a headscarf and not wearing tight and revealing clothes in the mosque, I gained access to work with the girls in the women's quarter.

Later in the study, in the settings outside the mosque, I had to mediate the difference between my ways of embodying modesty with that of the fathers. For example, one time while having tea Dojua's father in his restaurant, Marrakesh, we had an extensive discussion about "the" headscarf—which he referred to as "al *hijab*" I explained my position by stating that "the" headscarf is not obligatory for Muslim women to wear. That is, it is not one of the pillars of Islam and that it has been misinterpreted and misused. Dojua's father tried to persuade me that I was wrong and quickly called the imam (one who leads a group prayer) of the local mosque. Suddenly, he handed me his cell phone. I heard the imam shouting, "200%, yes, it is a must on Muslim women to wear the headscarf."

Despite my fear of revealing my contradictory position on to "veil or not to veil" with Dojua's father, and thus, creating an opening for him to judge me as not being modest enough, I quoted the most recited *hijab* verse,

O Prophet! say to your wives and your daughters and the women of the believers that to draw [a part] of their cloaks [jalābīhinna] close around them; that is more suitable, so that they will not be recognised and annoyed; and Allah is Forgiving, Merciful. (The Qur'an, 33:59)

Then I began explaining how it is misinterpreted because it is not contextualized (Mernissi, 1991). I said to him,

A headscarf in its modern form was introduced by the Ottomans and not by the Prophet. It was used by French and British colonizers in Algeria and Egypt to control the indigenous population through the body of Muslim women. This trapped Muslim men into controlling women's bodies further to assert their Muslim identity as a strategy to resist the Western colonizers throughout the past two hundred years. And by the way, head covering was also a tradition Christian and Jewish women followed for centuries before Islam.

By the end of this conversation, Dojua's father was at least in agreement with me that Muslim women's modesty should not come only through a scrap of cloth. However, he emphasized that he would still like to see Dojua wear a headscarf but would not pressure her to do so. I felt after this conversation that regardless of our difference on the meaning of modesty in dress, he still respected my perspective and continued to allow me to work with Dojua. That is, using my literacies of the history of the "veil" in the Orientalist discourses and *hijab* Qur'anic verses opened a conversation about the difference between my stand on modesty in dress and that of Dojua's father. This conversation mediated alternative meanings of modesty between us and brought about more chances for me to gain access to the lives of the four Muslim girls in this project.

HARAM

In Arabic, *haram* is the noun derived from the verb *hrm*, the opposite of what it allowed, *halal*, permissible (*Lisan Al 'Arab*). *Haram* means that which is forbidden by God (*Lisan Al 'Arab*). But *haram* is what is made sacred and safe like the premise of the mosque or one's private space. *Al hurmah* is what/who is not allowed to be violated or not allowed to be permissible. *Al hareem* is what/who a man protects such as a woman who is only allowed to be with her husband and is forbidden to be with any other man. Additionally, the most common use of the term *haram* applies to certain forbidden practices such as eating pork, drinking alcohol,[5] using drugs, socializing in coed spaces (the spatial *hijab*, and pursuing sexual or intimate encounters outside marriage (the ethical *hijab*).

Haram as the forbidden practices emerged as the fourth marker of difference between the parents and myself and challenged my eligibility to gain entry. The most crucial incident in which *haram* emerged was at the beginning of the first stage of this study. Right after my first visit to the Al Hilal mosque and upon the request of the head teacher, I called the head of the mosque council. Accordingly, I sent an official letter to the all-male mosque's council in which I requested their official permission to have the mosque as the site of the research study. In this letter, I presented the purpose of the study "is to understand how Muslim girls experience their bodily learning experiences." I listed the main methods of the study such as, "conversations, open-ended interviews, and journal writing, which will center on topics related to their health and physical activities provided in school or outside school (i.e., swimming, aerobics, kickboxing, gymnastics, and athletics)." Additionally, I listed the study's potential benefits to the girls and the community,

Each girl will have a better understanding of her health and well being as a Muslim girl in U.S. public schools; and knowledge gained will be used to help teachers relate better to Muslim girls with the hope of providing them with more just and equitable educational opportunities.

Next, the head of the council called me to clarify a few issues in order to facilitate the council's members' decision signing the official permission, a prerequisite to submitting the study's proposal application to the institutional review board of my university. He wanted to know what I meant in the letter by "the health and well-being" of the girls and was concerned about the methods of the study. He thought that by not using survey questions to review before hand, there was a chance the topic of sex would be encountered, "If you are only going to converse with the girl, will you be talking to them about sex." Bringing out sex, a *haram*, as a matter of "health and well-being" or as a bodily learning experience meant that the council would not approve my presence in the mosque with the girls. Accordingly, I explained to the head of the council the positive capabilities of open-ended interviews and conversation in working with young girls compared to predesigned questionnaires. I also assured him that I had no intention in talking about anything that is considered *haram* especially sex and sexual behavior. At the end of this phone conversation, he seemed satisfied and very cooperative. He promised to mail me the approval letter the next week after talking to all the council's members.

This was the first junction at which the full disclosure of the nature and the purpose of the study first surfaced and with it the difference over the *harams* emerged as another challenge to gain entry. The same night, I sent the head of the council an e-mail in which I reworded the purpose of the study to eliminate misconceptions on crossing the *harams*, talking about sex, and emphasized the benefits of the study to the girls. I described the study in a nonacademic and nonambiguous language highlighting physical activities rather than *bodily* experiences as the focus of the study, which later proved sufficient for approval (Lieblich, Tuval-Mashiach, & Zilber, 1998). My responsiveness to the mosque's council request not to be talking about sex, as *haram*, and making a change in the language used to reflect the purpose and the benefits of the study, were sufficient to gain approval for my entry. Six weeks later, and after days of phoning I finally met the head of the council to take the signed approval letter which allowed me to enter the women's quarters of the mosque and meet with the girls attending Sunday lessons. Consequently, the site of the first stage of the study was confirmed as the women's quarter of the local mosque. It was the only mosque in Al Hilal at the time of the pilot study.

Before I could spend time with the girls, the parents had to approve every new activity or location to make sure it was not *haram*. The parents wanted to ensure that none of the study's activities and sites presented a chance for their daughters to commit a *haram*. Their approval was conditional to one activity or one place at a time and it only stood valid until that activity was over. Early in the summer of 2006 while setting the schedule of activities for the study, Dojua's mother, Khatima, came to the university's activity center in order to check out the physical activities I planned for the study. She was representing the other three mothers; only two of them visited the activity center in the spring. Specifically prior to signing the parents' consent forms, she was responsible to ensure that none of the physical activities violated the visual, spatial and/or ethical *hijabs*, in other words were not *haram*. At this time, I showed her the wall-climbing room, the weightlifting room, the bike spinning room, and the pool facilities.

Khatima observed a wall-climbing class and a spinning class. In the wall-climbing class, she saw a male instructor touching the students' bodies while helping them to put a harness around their hips. She expressed that she did not want her daughter to join a wall-climbing class because of the physical proximity of the male instructor to the bodies of his students. In the spinning class, she saw that the majority of the participants were male lead by a female instructor. However, she did not mind the spinning classes when she said, "Well, I guess it is like being in school with boys. No problem." To Khatima, if the girls in this study took up wall climbing, they would be violating at least the one *haram* or the spatial *hijab* that is supposed to physically separate Muslim men from women in public spaces. However, Khatima flexibly read the presence of males in the spinning class as not so much a violation of a *haram*.

Additionally, when this same mother visited the indoor and outdoor pools and saw it was a coed space, she suggested that I take permission for the girls to swim in the indoor pool solely at least without the presence of males. She made this suggestion to avoid the potential violation of the *harams* or crossing the three *hijabs*, the visual, spatial, and ethical. She was concerned that in this case the girls may violate the *harams* if they wore anything more revealing other than their faces in the presence of males.

The possibility of violating the *haram* in at least three physical activities—wall climbing, spinning, and swimming—before even beginning the study was discouraging for me. I was also concerned that taking time to negotiate the *harams* with every single mother would also delay the start of the study. Within a week after Khatima's tour of the activity center, I visited all four mothers. In these visits, I intended to understand how these mothers interpreted the *harams* in relation to the physical activities offered in the study and accordingly find ways to make these activities possible for their daughters. Extensively, I discussed the benefits of physical activities to their girls and asked for their input on solutions that would not violate the *harams*. I called all four mothers and offered to provide the girls with a female wall-climbing instructor and to obtain a permission for the girls to override the dress code at the university pool and swim with long pants instead of a swimsuit and/or while keeping on the headscarf. Immediately after, two mothers returned the signed consent forms with their daughters.

Another junction of negotiating the *haram* was related to Layla, who wore a headscarf and had the most difficulty with her father "policing" every move she wanted to make outside home or school. On the third Saturday we met, Layla invited me to visit her house. She wanted me to meet her father in order to facilitate his consent to the particulars of the study, and thus, assure her weekly participation with the group. At this point though presented with an opportunity to review and hopefully sign the consent form in person, I apologized knowing that I needed to clear my way first with the mother and make sure she would be present too. That week, I arranged with Layla's mother to visit them at home the next Saturday morning when I picked Layla up. Once more, I knew better that being present with a man alone in one space, private or public, is *haram* (Ahmed, 1992; Mernissi, 1991). While the urgency to sign the consent form was weighing heavily on me, I could have made a serious mistake costing me the trust of Layla's mother. In other words, if I had accepted to meet Layla's father without his wife's presence, another adult female from the family, could have reflected my ignorance of the *harams* and consequently denied me access to at least Layla's life or her participation in the study.

After spending time with Layla, Dojua, Abby, and Amy and conversing with them about their favorite physical activities, favorite school subjects, ways they spend their time after school, I learned about some of the more obvious *harams*, these girls had to negotiate in their lives. They included: (1) exercising and swimming in public with the presence of boys; (2) wearing clothes of their choice; (3) dating boys; (4) talking about sex or watching movies with sex scenes; (5) going to parties that included dancing; (6) visiting their non-Muslim friends; (7) traveling with the school sports teams; (8) driving a car alone; (9) staying out after dark; (10) attending football games; and (11) shopping at the mall without their mothers.

Occasionally, I had to cancel some of the study's activities in order to demonstrate to the parents that I respected their request that their girls not participate in any activity that could be considered *haram*. Thus, I constantly had to design new tasks or modify the planned tasks of the study in response to the parents' last minute approval or denial of a potentially *haram* activity. My early recognition of the *harams* and my quick responsiveness to change the activities of the study assured the participation of the girls, and thus, helped me maintained my continual access to their lives. For example, early in the spring and before starting the formal study I was afraid that the parents might deny the girls to participate in the second part of the study because of the presence of males in the university activities center. However, after the visit and after meeting my advisor, the mothers seemed to approve of the space and were excited about the prospects of engaging their daughters with fun and useful activities during the summer break.

In the above examples, I recognized and negotiated even the subtle *harams* that blocked or delayed entry and kept access conditional. Again, my literacies of how the *harams* permeate implicitly in Muslims' everyday activities and my flexibility in responding to them not only assured the signing of consent forms by the parents at the beginning but also kept me from losing access into the lives of these girls.

SUMMARY

In this chapter, I discussed how the process of gaining research access into the lives of Layla, Dojua, Abby, and Amy, the four Muslim girls in this study, was pivotal to gaining access and maintaining entry in this research project. Specifically, I discussed the challenges that included, (1) being Muslim enough, (2) *inshallah* (Allah or God willing), (3) being modest enough, and (4) *haram* (forbidden). These challenges were markers of difference on both *muslimness* and the interpretations of the *hijabs* and the *hijab* discourse between the girls, the parents, and myself. The four challenges were markers of difference on both *muslimness* and the interpretations of the *hijabs* and the *hijab* discourse between the girls, the parents, and myself.

What follows are the main stories of this study about the girls' stories of *deveiling* the *hijabs*.

CHAPTER 5

DEVEILING THE *HIJABS*

The coach in my school always nags me to join the basketball and volleyball teams. See I am tall and my brother is a great basketball player. But my father says I cannot play because I am a girl and besides he says that I will be looking like a monkey running up and down the court [giggles] making a show for the boys in my school. (Layla, 16)

I love swimming. I was starting to win competitions in this city but last year mom pulled me out. She thought Karate is good for me so I am not swimming anymore. I like Karate but I want to swim too.... She tells me because I am Muslim I cannot wear a swimsuit. But I wear shorts for PE [laughs] but long shorts. I don't know. (Amy, 14)

In this chapter I discuss how three *hijabs*—visual, spatial and ethical—acted as a central gendering discourse in the lives of Layla, Dojua, Abby, and Amy, the four Muslim girls who participated in the study. The girls conformed to their parents' interpretations of three *hijabs*, in their dress, social activities and physical activities, and movement in public. They also questioned them and finally *deveiled* them to cross the fourth spiritual *hijab*. In spaces and moments outside the reach of the *hijab* discourse, the girls renarrated themselves, as Muslim girls. They called for teachers to pay attention to them with their differences, and, with their similarities to other girls their age in U.S. public schools.

In the following, I map three main themes, (1) enforcing; (2) questioning; and (3) *deveiling* the *hijabs*—visual, spatial, ethical, and the spiritual. As a reminder for the reader, the *hijab* according to Mernissi (1991) is four-dimensional—visual, spatial, ethical, and spiritual. The Arabic verb

Pedagogies of Deveiling: Muslim Girls and the Hijab Discourse,
pp. 87–111

hjb, means to cover, hide, shelter, protect, and establish a barrier, border, screen, or threshold (Mernissi, 1991). That is, the *hijab* (noun) is not only the visual representation of a headscarf, the cloth that hides Muslim females' bodies from the male gaze. It is also the spatial *hijab*, the walls that shelter Muslim females out of public spaces; the ethical *hijab*, the limits that protect them from the forbiddens, *harams*, like physical/sexual encounters with males; and the spiritual *hijab*, the ignorance that blinds Muslim from deeper knowledge (Mernissi, 1991).

ENFORCING THE *HIJABS*

> The reason I do wear [the headscarf] sometimes is to please my parents.... You are not supposed to make your body for men to see so they will think about bad things about you or know you by your body. (Layla, 17)

The girls' parents' positions to the visual, spatial, and ethical *hijabs* dominated the girls' talk and action throughout the study. The parents' different interpretations and degrees of enforcing the three *hijabs* or veils—the visual, spatial, and ethical—emerged, (1) at the introduction of the study to the parents; (2) at the introduction of the physical activities made available in the study; and (3) in the girls' private journals. As I illustrate in the following stories, Layla, Dojua, Abby, and Amy were instructed and monitored to conform to their parents' interpretations of the three *hijabs*. Both the mothers and the fathers challenged the girls' ways of dressing, places they wanted to go to, and people and activities they were interested in. Though initially, each parent's interpretation of the *hijabs* determined the kind of physical activities and the public spaces that were made available to the girls; these interpretations were diverse and negotiated during the first 4 months of the study.

Dressing Modestly: "I am Muslim I Cannot Wear a Swimsuit"

The girls' parents enforced the practice of the visual *hijab* in public every time they were going out. At times, the parents enforced the girls' modest dress in subtle ways hinting to them what they should wear before leaving the house and other times in very direct and harsh ways telling them exactly what not to wear. Though Layla was the only one wearing a headscarf and all four girls wore contemporary teenage fashion, *all* four girls were consistently instructed and monitored to dress modestly.

The range of the parents' interpretations of the visual *hijab* was additionally reflected by the diversity of the mothers' embodiments of the visual *hijab*. That is, the starting point from which each girl was allowed to dress modestly in public or how much she was supposed to "cover" or could "reveal" of her body was partially shaped by the flexibility of her own mother's embodiment of the visual *hijab*. While Dojua, Amy, and Abby, did not wear a headscarf, their mothers embodied the visual *hijab* differently. Layla's and Dojua's mother wore the headscarf in public. Amy's mother loosely wrapped her head and neck with a very thin white or colored scarf and only when she was around men in public. Abby's mother covered her hair only at prayer. Moreover, in the second half of the study, Layla's father was trying to impose a stricter visual *hijab* on her, the headscarf as well as the *jilbab*[1] (as Layla called it). This change in Layla's father's interpretation of the visual *hijab* signaled a potential threat to her overall mobility in public, and consequently to her participation in the project's activities even further.

Every Saturday before leaving the house with me, each mother or father inspected her/his daughter's modesty in dress. On more than one occasion, Dojua's mother would ask her to clean off her face makeup before leaving the house and Amy's mother would go to her room to check what she was wearing before leaving. On the last day of the study, we all witnessed how Abby's father harshly gestured to her before leaving the house to go and change the clothes she had chosen.

When swimming at the university pool was presented as an optional activity in the study, Dojua's mother informed me that she would allow her daughter to swim if she were in an area far from males' sight and if "Dojua will wear something like long shorts and a long sleeve shirt." Wanting the girls not to miss out on the opportunities provided by the study and allowing me to negotiate the *hijabs*, this same mother suggested that I should look into having the girls access the indoor swimming pool without the presence of males.

Layla, who was the only girl wearing the headscarf at the time, expressed that she was prohibited from swimming—and certainly wearing a swimsuit—not only because she was a girl and had to cover her head but also because she was Muslim. She wrote in her journal that her father told her, "Public pools are dirty for Muslims to swim in." Wearing a swimsuit for Layla was not negotiable since she was already wearing a headscarf and battling her father's new orders to wear the *jilbab* too. Abby had no problem with any of the conditions inscribed on the other three girls and was apparently allowed to swim with her two-piece bathing suit.

Though Amy loved swimming and was winning competitions the previous year she was prohibited from wearing a swimsuit. She wrote in her journal, "I was starting to win competitions in this city but last year mom pulled me out. She tells me because I am Muslim I cannot wear a swimsuit. I am not swimming anymore." However, Amy's mother showed some flexibility on how Amy could embody the visual *hijab* at the university pool, when she said, "Amy is 14 and can still enjoy swimming." What her mother meant was that Amy was not at the age yet where she would be forbidden to swim in public. For now Amy could wear a light shirt and long thick surfing shorts.

Unsegregated Gender Physical Activities/Spaces: "My Father Says I Cannot Play Basketball Because I am a Girl"

The girls' parents enforced the spatial *hijab* on several places. Additionally, the parents' veiling-off spaces were complicated by the target activity in each space and by its potential to violate the visual and ethical *hijabs* as well. Football games, public pools, and dancing parties were some of the spaces that were veiled-off from Layla, Dojua, Abby, and Amy. Layla and Dojua were restricted from going to football games, even school games. All four girls were prohibited from going to parties, spending the night at houses of friends who were not Muslim, or any place associated with boys and/or with alcohol. They were all prohibited from staying out of the house after dark, as Layla said, "When I do go out and come back after staying out all day, he [her father] gets mad, he hates it when I go out and keep going or stay after hours."

For fear of violating the spatial *hijab*, Layla, Dojua, and Abby were not allowed to spend the night at a friend's house. However occasionally, Amy was allowed to spend the night at her best friend's house because firstly, there were no men in the family and, secondly, her friend's mother as Amy said, "understands the Muslim thing." In this situation, since there were no men in the house, there was no threat that Amy would violate the spatial *hijab*. However, Layla, Dojua, and Abby were forbidden from going to houses of girlfriends who were not Muslim even for day visits. Since men and boys may be present, the girls' parents did not trust that any of the *hijabs* would not be "taken off or crossed." Abby expressed how her opportunities of making friends who are not Muslim became more and more limited due to her parents' particular interpretation of the spatial *hijab*. Moreover, she had limited opportunities to maintain and/or make Muslim friends because she lived in a town with a small Muslim community.

> I do not have Muslim friends though. We don't talk to them any more because one is living in another city she moved and the other one her whole

family stopped going to the mosque. We still talk online sometime but like I haven't seen her in 2 years. (Abby)

Overall, these girls, unlike their brothers even those who were younger, stayed home unless chaperoned to and from a work place or chaperoned at an extra-curricular activity after school. While Layla and Abby have a driver's license, they were seldom if ever allowed to drive alone. Layla was allowed to drive herself to school but not to classes at the nearby community college. The other times when the girls had to go to places related to their formal schooling, an adult or male figure from the family had to escort them. Particularly, Layla and Abby often had to have their older brothers as their main and constant escorts. Amy on the other hand, was allowed to attend the home coming football game of her school only because her mother trusted Manal as another legitimate escort. Abby traveled last year with her schools' football team over the weekend to a northern city in her state. She was the team's assistant trainer at the time. Her father allowed her to travel only accompanied by her older brother. Similarly, Layla was only occasionally allowed to go to certain public places if her brother was escorting her.

Abby, Amy, and Dojua were allowed to swim in public pools as long as they wore the modest swimming attire their mothers prescribed. However, Layla was not allowed to put on any swim attire and all together was not allowed to be in a public pool. Her father told her, "Public pools are dirty for Muslims to swim in." This implied that the dipping/swimming in public water was forbidden for Layla as a Muslim, and at the same time, it implied that the pool area is a place that violates all of the three *hijabs*. However, when the time arrived to go to the pool, Layla's mother allowed her to join the girls as long as she kept her headscarf on while sitting at the edge of the pool and dipping her legs in the water.

Layla expressed her blocked desire to join her schools' basketball and volleyball teams and explained, "My father says I cannot play because I am a girl and besides he says that I will be making a show for the boys in my school." This restriction on Layla to play basketball in school is not only an expression of her father's interpretation of the visual and spatial *hijabs* but also an emphasis of her mother's fear of her befriending African American boys. That is, restricting Layla from her favorite physical activity reflects the interpretation of the three *hijabs* simultaneously.

Befriending Boys: "She Freaks Out if I Talk to Him"

The girls' parents enforced the ethical *hijab* by challenging the girls' socialization with/around boys in school spaces and during any extracurricular activity. That is, spending time with boys alone, being around boys in a gender nonsegregated space, dating, and befriending boys would be considered breaking or crossing the ethical *hijab* as well as the spatial *hijab*.

At the beginning of the study, all of the girls expressed their liking for boys but as far as I knew throughout the study; none of them were dating. On more than one occasion, Layla shared with us that being Muslim and liking African American boys, whom she called "Dudes" was problematic to her parents. Her mother never allowed her to be around them even if they were her brothers' friends. She said, "because my mother acts like psycho around Dudes ... like she knows I am crazy about Blacks." The girls backed her up expressing how befriending boys and dating conflicted with their parents' *hijabs*.

> Abby: It is just he [her father] thinks that like I am gonna go get pregnant or something if I talk to a guy I swear.
>
> Layla: My mom thinks so [that she will sleep with boys], that is why she is like psycho.
>
> Amy: My mom does think that too.

The girls also explained that their parents' *hijabs* in this example meant that they were not allowed to have relationships with boys before marriage—which may be a concern of any parent who is not Muslim too. However, this prohibition was particularly extended to having friendships with boys who were not Muslim. This was revealed in the following conversations:

> Abby: It is because they are not Muslim, isn't it?
>
> Layla: Well that is true if I think about it.
>
> Abby: If they were Muslim they think oh that is nice and since they are not Muslim they are bad or there is no point in pursuing a relationship with him.
>
> Layla: Exactly.
>
> Abby: Because we cannot even get married to them.

One day, when the girls were creating their individual scrapbooks and were filling them up with many images and photos of both males and females, Abby showed her apprehension about sharing her work with her parents. She said, "Are our parents going to see this?" When I assured her that it would be confidential, she continued, "OK, good because I do not want my parents to see this [pointing to a photo of a young boy]." So, when I probed and tried to learn more, she revealed that she liked an older boy who was an African American football player. She hung out with him after school because as she said, "He is nice;" however she added, "My dad does not like him." A moment later Abby shared that her father, a school district math consultant, would drop in any time at her school, especially after classes and check on who she was hanging out with and what she was doing.

In the above examples of the beginning of the study, the girls' conformity to the parents' own interpretations of the *hijabs* was evident. They seemed to be coerced and even fearful of questioning the authority of the Qur'an, the main source they thought that legitimated the parents' *hijabs*. Layla who wore the headscarf since she was 11, wrote in the first pages of her journal, "the reason I do wear it sometimes is to please my parents ... I have told my mother I don't want to wear it, but she feels it is her responsibility to make me and I have to honor her." While Layla's age and respect for her mother compelled her to wear the headscarf, she had no room to question anything about it even though she did "not feel ready to wear a *hijab* [headscarf]" and did "not feel any different when [she was] wearing it and when [she was] not." Additionally, she wrote that her mother asked her neither "to argue the Qur'an" nor to question her father's orders to wear the *jilbab*. However, as the study progressed, each of the girls started to question the *hijabs*.

QUESTIONING THE *HIJABS*

In the Qur'an, it doesn't say it's not *haram* to date. It just says there should be no physical contact between men and woman before marriage. (Amy, 14)

Gradually, Layla, Dojua, Abby, and Amy started using the time we spent together, as well as their journaling, as open spaces for questioning and discussing their parents' particular interpretations of the *hijabs*. As we moved on and in the bigger group conversations, they were questioning their parents' reasoning behind reinforcing some sort of modest dress, prohibiting them from going to football games, and forbidding dating.

Troubling the Modest Dress: "Does the Headscarf Prevent Men From Thinking 'Bad Things'?"

In their journals and while listening to their music in the privacy of the study room, the girls questioned the visual *hijab* represented in the modesty of dress and wearing a headscarf. They questioned their parents fixed notions of the visual *hijab* by trying to make sense, for example by responding to the outsiders gaze and explaining it to their school peers. Layla wrote in her journal about her struggle with what the visual *hijab* meant to her since she had worn the headscarf for the past 6 years,

> When I was 11 it [the headscarf] really bothered me, I did not want to go out ... when I was young I was like "why are they looking at me" ... I faced the changes of this age and the scarf too ... [freshman year] I was with my brother and everybody would just look at me. I would always be with my brother and they are just always looking and then some of them like "can I ask you a personal question?" then they will ask me why I am wearing it then I explain like "because of religion." Then when they ask more like I say, "you are supposed to be covering up. You are not supposed to make your body for men to see so they will think about bad things about you or know you by your body more than your face or your personality" and then they like "oh that is pretty cool that is cool."

Additionally, Abby and Dojua problematized their parents' interpretations of the visual *hijab* especially by exposing their fathers' reasoning behind inspecting their way of dressing in public. Abby said, "He knows what all guys think about," and Dojua followed, "it is because all Arab guys are like that, protective." This moment presented to me an opening to invite Layla to question what she wrote earlier, which seemed consistent with what Abby and Dojua were starting to discuss. I used Layla's words and said, "But do you think that the scarf prevents men from thinking 'bad things' when they look at a woman with a headscarf?" Layla expressed maybe a glimpse of critiquing the *hijabs* and answered, "No, I really don't." I continued to probe and said, "Right, how come?" At this moment, Layla might have started to see how men sexualized her body when they look at her whether she is wearing the headscarf or not, as she said, "Because they will still see it."

Later in the conversation more of this subtle critique emerged when Layla told us how her father prohibited her from going out with one of her school friend's who was not Muslim because of how he had "seen the way she dresses." Layla continued to question her father's interpretation of her friend's dress and thus his prohibition of her to maintain the friendship. She told him, "But she is like my friend ... I did not understand it. I was like 'I am not going to go dress like that, she is just my friend.'" As Layla was trying to make sense of her father's judgment of her friend and her way of dressing, I asked, "How does she dress?" She answered with sheer puzzlement in her voice, "Like a normal American girl, like tight jeans and tight shirts." I was puzzled too and asked, "But you wear tight jeans and tight shirts too!" Layla answered, "Yeah, I did not understand ... I was confused more confused."

Unpacking the Prohibitions on Going to Football Games: "I Don't Drink so What Is the Big Deal?"

The girls questioned the spatial *hijabs* in several occasions. For example, we were all discussing Dojua's parents' decision prohibiting her from going to a football game at Abby's school—even if I escorted her. They expressed their confusion behind the reasoning for this prohibition. Dojua said, "Sometimes they confuse me but I don't think this time it is because of boys." When I asked Dojua's mother about her decision for next Saturday's plans, she said, "We just don't like our girls going to such events like football games." In this example, since Dojua did not think the males' presence in football games was the only reason for her parents' disapproval, I speculated that Dojua's mother thought of alcohol as the forbidden ethical *hijab* behind her decision and that it was overlapping with the spatial *hijab* in this case. When I suggested that to Dojua, she said, "I don't drink so what is the big deal?" On another occasion, I learned that Dojua's mother never attended a football game and when I suggested that I would be happy to accompany her to one of Dojua's school football games, she politely refused. In this example, again Dojua told us how she was struggling to make sense of the conflicts between her desires to socialize in places outside her school circle and her parents' interpretation of the spatial *hijab*.

Later on the same day and on the way back from Al Jiser, the girls continued this discussion to reveal more of how they were struggling to make sense of their parents' spatial *hijabs* and how they eventually—and maybe temporarily—submitted to the restrictions on places, activities, and people they could be experiencing. Layla clarified,

> My mom was okay with it when I told her. But my dad is the same way as Dojua's parents like about games, like he will not let me go though one time and he let me go with my brother, so I think he is a little more OK with it than Dojua's dad.

In this, Layla was also struggling with the spatial *hijab*. She however accepted the minor privilege her father offered her by having her brother escort her. The brother in this case was supposed to be acting as both the visual and spatial *hijab* in public places to keep the gaze of men away from Layla's body. At the same time, he acted as the ethical *hijab* to deter her from interacting with boys. Layla struggled with these meanings of the *hijabs*, which reflected her parents' mistrust in her ability to make her own decisions about her body. She said, "I usually do not question it because I see why he makes rules. I hate them but I understand from his point of view he is over protective." Layla's mother did not permit her to go to a school football game even if escorted by her brother, as she said, "My dad is okay with it, it is my mom 'god why do you want to go, you are not going to even watch the game' that's what she thinks."

Struggling With the Forbiddens: "I Heard in Islam it Is Not *Haram* (Forbidden) to Date?"

In several discussions, the girls questioned the ethical *hijab* that forbade them from dating and socializing with boys. The girls were trying to figure out how dating was *haram* to them as Muslim girls and to what extent, and whom would they date or not date and why. Their conversations showed that they each had a different meaning to dating.

Amy: Well you know I heard in Islam it is not *haram* (forbidden) to date, like you guys are all happy.

Abby: What? But dating does not have to do with being a virgin [protecting one's virginity].

Amy: No it is like like if you are in college or something and like you are serious about getting married to a person it is okay to date them.

Abby: But you cannot date a guy who is not Muslim though.

Amy: I am not saying a Muslim.

Layla: Hay, but that is not fair Muslim men can date non-Muslim women and my mom says it is "because the man is the head of the house hold."

Abby: No, it is because it used to be that because the children will grow up not Muslim that is if a woman is married to a non-Muslim guy the child will grow up non-Muslim something like that.

Layla: Yeah, but what if a non-Muslim male converts into a Muslim? What happens?

Abby: Did you hear the story? This non-Muslim guy was dating a Muslim girl to shut up the parents, he showed up at the mosque and he like converted then he asked her to marry him and then she tells her mother who like "that is not right" and now they are dating anyways. *I think this is stupid.* (Shouting)

Layla: That is why you cannot marry a non-Muslim, because non-Muslims are into drugs and alcohol.

Manal: Is that why? Does this mean your mom was doing that too before she converted and married your father?

Layla: Yeah, I know, that is why I do not understand.

Manal: Dojua, suppose you start to like somebody a lot and he likes you a lot, what happens? Do you stop yourself?

Layla: It is hard.

Abby: I don't knoooooooooooow.

Dojua: You cannot. It is like I don't know.

Manal: Does it make the guy you like less of a good guy and less loving and less respecting to you if he is not Muslim?

Layla: No.

Dojua: No I think they would be more respectful.

Layla: I agree.

Dojua: If they are Muslim they are like not supposed to be doing that, like stupid.

Abby: But then you tell them [I am Muslim] and they are like "well."

Dojua: They say religion does not matter.

Layla added: If it is a guy who likes me and wants to talk to me a lot he tries to look into the religion [Islam].

Two weeks later, I asked Amy in her journal about dating, and I wrote, "Explain to me how it is not *haram* to date in Islam? Or what would Muslim dating look like for you?" Amy wrote back,

In the Qur'an, it doesn't say it's not *haram* to date. It just says there should be no physical contact between men and woman before marriage. I think Islamic dating would be around the age of 18, when you are older and more mature, so you wouldn't just date a guy, because of his looks. It would be dating with a lot more respect.

In a later conversation, the group questioning the ethical *hijab* and dating continued,

Amy: Some people only think of sex but like you can date without sex. Like most people in this country when they think of dating like say non-Muslim yeah they assume it is all about sex, but like it is not, it is like you can have a relationship with respect.

Manal: What about holding hands or kissing.

Amy: Well people are different like you should be like older like you know older mature and not like 12 years old and like you know what I mean.

Manal: But what is dating then?

Amy: Well now people like dating like bonding like it is just a game they date one then another. It is like really rare to find people that like in a love relationship like 2 years or 3 years like mostly like "oh I yeah I went out with him for a week and broke up with him."

Manal: So do you think you are old enough to date?

Amy: I don't think I am [she is 14].

Dojua: I don't think she is old enough for love.

Manal: But how will you know?

Amy: I think you will know like when you are mature and like like everybody is like "I am mature I know I am."

Abby: Ninety percent of the times you go out with some guy you have no idea about them. Seriously if you think about everybody that starts going out has no idea about the person they are going out with.

Amy: Unless you are really like he is one of your really good friends.

Abby: But usually you don't want to go out with someone you have a good friendship with and you don't know what happens.

Layla: A lot of times people do that.

Amy: I think dating is to get to know each other.

Layla: And sometimes you regret it and it is not worth it.

Dojua: When someone were in love they would do whatever it takes just to be with that person, and religion or parents are not going to stop it, right? It is the love, both of them are in love and like like truly like there are no doubts about any of the love or anything and they like being with each and like no one can stop them not even religion or their parents.

Amy: Cause like love like when you think about it, it is really a strong word not like oh yeah just telling anybody "I love you."

As the girls continued to question the ethical *hijab* on dating, Layla and Abby explained that their fathers prohibited them from befriending boys because as,

Abby explained: My father tells me that he knows what all guys think about.

Dojua clarified: It is because all Arab guys are like that, protective.

Abby shouted to explain further, why her father thinks why boys were not to be trusted.

He just says "once I was a boy, or I was younger once, I know what they think about." He means they [boys] think about sex. He thinks all guys all they think about is getting in your pants.

Though the parents' interpretations of the *hijabs* conflicted with the girls' expressed desires to dress as they pleased, go anywhere they chose, and enjoy boys' friendships and/or dating, Layla, Dojua, Abby, and Amy kept their questioning alive and began experimenting with ways to expose and deveil all of the three *hijabs*.

DEVEILING THE HIJABS

When I jumped in the pool fully clothed, [it] was something I will never regret. When I did that I felt like I threw the rule book out the window! (Layla, 17)

As we moved through the study, the girls shared and illustrated their strategies of how they exposed and deveiled the visual, spatial and ethical *hijabs* and their consequential restrictions on their learning. In the safe spaces and activities made available in this study, they deveiled their parents' interpretation of these three *hijabs*, consequentially, crossed the spiritual *hijab*. In this *deveiling* process, the girls did not stop at critiquing the *hijabs* but they began to open possibilities of reinterpreting or resisting the *hijabs* altogether. As a start, the girls deveiled the *hijabs* by redesigning the modesty of their dress, swimming in a public pool, participating in several enjoyable physical activities, and befriending boys. The girls' *deveiling* strategies included their smart arguments with their parents, use of me as a legitimate escort, and selection of enjoyable physical activities.

More critically, this meant that by the end of the 14-month long study, Layla, Dojua, Abby, and Amy crossed the fourth spiritual *hijab*. In spaces and moments outside the reach of the *hijab* discourse, the girls renarrated themselves, as *muslim* girls, to an outsider through a conversation around making a body collage and scrapbooks. They storied their multiple selves; in images, quotes, jokes, and words.

Redesigning the Modest Dress: "I Would Have Fought Him— It Is Just You Were There"

The girls redesigned the visual *hijab* in the way they dressed throughout the study. The clothing combination that Dojua and Amy chose reflected their own interpretation of the visual *hijab* complicated by the diverse interpretations of their parents. In the following examples, it was evident that the girls knew when and how to dress the way they wanted away from their parents' direct monitoring and how to confront them if necessary.

Every week when I picked up Layla, she dressed in her modest clothes—the long headscarf covering her upper body and the loose long overjacket or the baggy clothes. As soon as we were a few miles away from her house, heading towards campus or Al Jiser, and while still in the car, Layla took off the headscarf and let her long hair loose or she took off the overjacket to keep her teenage stylish outfit and the headscarf. At times, she put some makeup on, took off the headscarf, and kept her baggy clothes on. Other times, she kept the headscarf but wore teenage fashion outfits where more of her skin was revealed. Sometimes, Layla wore a half cut shirt showing her belly especially if she was at the pool or playing basketball at the university's activity center, sometimes keeping on her headscarf and sometimes taking it off. Before leaving her house, Layla discretely tucked the extra clothes in her handbag, or she was already wearing the alternative outfit under the *modest* attire with which she left her house. Similarly, Dojua left the house without makeup but started to put it on as soon as we drove off. Both Layla and Dojua seemed aware of when and how to dress with modesty without violating their parents' interpretations of the *hijabs*.

The first time the girls went to the university pool, Layla had her headscarf on and a short-sleeved shirt and baggy sweat pants. Dojua wore a swimsuit with a very short tight skirt-like bottoms and a matching bra-top. Amy wore a sleeveless shirt with thin straps—showing her upper chest—and long and thin surfing shorts.

On the last day in the study, Abby shared how she usually resisted her father's visual *hijab* when he did not approve of her dress choice before going out. She said, "I would have fought him. It is just you were there and like he would have gotten all like butt hurt and everything." Abby decided this time not to confront her father's restrictions and negotiate his interpretations of the visual *hijab*. She usually would either argue her way out or simply dress the way she liked away from his direct monitoring.

Crossing the Forbidden Spaces and Selecting Enjoyable Physical Activities: "When I Jumped in the Pool Fully Clothed, [it] was Something I Will Never Regret"

The girls crossed the spatial and ethical *hijabs* by enjoying certain physical activities in nonsegregated gender spaces. The array of physical activities choices offered in this study and the sheer presence of the girls in the university activity center, presented the girls with another chance. Every Saturday when the girls joined me in the study room, they passed through the pool, the gym, the spinning and wall climbing rooms, and the basketball court. They also had over 6 hours to "play" after completing the formal 1–3 hours allocated for the study doing their scrap books, making the body collage and journaling.

Half way through the study over several weeks, the girls started to try the physical activities available at the university center. Independently, Dojua joined a spinning class while the rest of the girls watched. She did not last more than 10 minutes. She left telling us that she merely did not like it because, "the bike saddle is too painful." All four girls wanted to try wall climbing. However, not long after I laid out the gear for them to put on and before the female instructor arrived, Dojua said, "I don't like putting on these shoes on without socks … and I don't like this [harness] tying me down" and Amy said disgusted, "the shoes smell." They all left the room giggling.

When it was time to check out the weightlifting room and the cardio room, they spent a good time on the bikes and the treadmills but did not select this activity again. In the weight lifting room, I introduced to them the different stations and demonstrated to them some of the exercises. They tried a few exercises for a short while but they were mostly giggling, watching themselves on the mirrors, and peeking at the boys too. Again, they did not ask to weight lift again. Abby said, "it was too loud." After these trials, they all ended up independently choosing the physical activity they enjoyed whether we thought at the beginning it was prohibited by the parents or not. All this time, I was listening to the girls' impressions of trying new activities and kept reminding them of the remaining options.

The last third of the study, the girls decided to spend their "play" time in swimming and playing basketball. Layla and Abby seemed more interested in basketball while Amy and Dojua opted to sunbathe at the outdoor pool. Though being restricted from playing basketball in school, Layla played pick-up basketball with whoever was around at the university center. In one of the group conversations, Layla expressed that she was restricted from her favorite physical activity and from her desire to join her schools' basketball and volleyball teams. She said, "My father says I cannot play because I am a girl and besides he says that I will be making a show for the boys in my school." Layla was told that she must stay away from the basketball courts as a gender nonsegregated space and from showing her moving body to the male audience. This was an expression of Layla's father's visual and spatial *hijabs*.

The last five Saturdays of the study, the girls chose to spend their time at the university pool and illustrated their ways of crossing all of the three *hijabs*. The first time the girls went to the university pool, Layla had her headscarf on and a short-sleeved shirt and baggy sweat pants. Dojua wore a swimsuit with a very short tight skirt-like bottom and a matching bra top. Amy wore a sleeveless shirt with thin straps—showing her upper chest—and long and thin surfing shorts. None of the clothing combinations that Layla, Dojua, and Amy put on were much in compliance with their parents' dress rules prescribed earlier. By the end of the study, the girls wore what ranged between a two-piece swimsuit and a headscarf with short tank tops and long pants. As the study progressed and we were spending an extended time in the activity center, the girls used their "play" time alternating between swimming and playing basketball. More than five times, the girls chose to swim in the university pool and lounge around in the sun even with the presence of men/boys—lifeguards and swimmers.

The first day we were at the university pool, initially the girls decided to use the indoor pool. Nobody was there except one female lifeguard; that is, there were no males present. Thus at that moment the clothing the girls were wearing did not violate the spatial dimension of the *hijab*. Layla and I sat on the side benches watching the other three girls swim with flippers and floaters. I was happy to finally see the girls having a chance to swim. A few minutes after the girls were in the water giggling and obviously having a good time, Dojua teasingly called Layla, "come and jump in." Layla screamed answering her immediately, "*I am going in!*" Quickly, she took off her bracelets and her colored contacts. I looked around and there were still no men in the area, and Layla said, "I will go in as I am and if a man comes in please let me know then I will put on my headscarf." Then suddenly she pulled off her headscarf and ran off jumping in the shallow end of the pool. For more than 20 minutes, the girls' giggles and sound of splashing filled the air. When the girls finally decided to move to the outdoor pool and Layla walked to the locker room to change her soaking wet clothes, I saw a male lifeguard coming on duty at the indoor pool. The timing of the lifeguard switch from female to male was fortunate for the girls because the spatial *hijab* would have been violated if the switch had happened while they were still in the indoor pool premises.

A few minutes later, Layla walked out of the locker room to the outdoor pool with a big towel wrapped around her and her black scarf loosely wrapped around her head while carrying her dripping clothes. Layla approached the girls and they started giggling. Dojua, Abby, and Amy were already on the lounges sunbathing. Amy stood up to help Layla squeeze dry her clothes and said "You look like Muslim women from Dubai." They all laughed again. The girls already knew that there were different embodiments of the visual *hijab* in different Muslim countries and contexts and now they were experiencing a few of their own.

With her big fashionable sunglasses, Layla lounged back on a sunbathing chair and covered the rest of her legs with a towel and pulled her black scarf around her head loosely while shading her face too. For the next 2 hours, I sat chatting with Layla while Dojua and Amy joined us between a few dips in the pool. Any time at a public swimming pool, there were two ways in which Layla had to be veiled-off by the spatial and the visual *hijabs*. First, Layla was forbidden to see the nudity of men and this meant not being in a swimming pool with them. Second, she had to wear her headscarf to prevent any man gazing at her body. However, Layla continued to wear long pants and a shirt, she still went into the water to swim with floaters.

Swimming at the university pool, was the particular space and the activity in which these girls continued to improvise in changing swimming outfits, further challenging all three *hijabs*. They later expressed that they had no regrets about having fun or about resorting to strategies of *develing*, reinterpreting and resisting, the *hijabs*. In her journal, Layla wrote, "Last Saturday when I jumped in the pool fully clothed, [it] was something I will never regret. When I did that I felt like I threw the rule book out the window!" Similarly, Dojua wrote, "Last week was pretty cool the best part was that Layla jumped in the pool when I told her. ☺ That was fun."

Befriending Boys: "I Told Him 'What Do you Want Me to Date Girls' Seriously 'What the Hell Do you Want Me to Do to Turn Gay or Something'?"

Each of the girls had one or more strategy of reinterpreting and resisting the ethical *hijab*, the *haram* of befriending boys. Layla shared her liking of African American boys by including in her scrapbook the photos of her favorite actors and hip-hop performers. She checked out the African American boys on the basketball courts, the gym, and on campus. Driving out of the activity center when Layla saw an African American young student, she asked me to slow down at the intersection, "Yeah take your time why don't you. He is very cute."

Later in the study and on one occasion, Layla surprised me by inviting some of her African American friends to the activity center for a basketball game. The same boys her mother did not allow her to play with even in the presence of her brother. Again, in the safe space this study provided the girls, Layla took the chance and independently decided to do what she would likely enjoy. That day for an hour, Abby and Layla played with whom Layla called "her Dudes" while Amy and Dojua were swimming. I sat for a while watching them, and it was clear that the guys liked Layla and that she was popular. When it was time to leave, they hugged Layla and thanked her for playing with them. I wrote in my field notes, "Layla is crossing the *hijabs* again and throwing more rules out the window." To Layla, keeping the headscarf on while playing with the boys who she considered her friends was not quite a violation to any of the ethical and spatial *hijabs* her parents prohibited her from violating.

Close to the end of the study, when the girls were still working on the scrapbooks in the study room, privately Abby shared with me her strategies of befriending boys.

> Abby: It is cause ummm my dad got mad cause he saw us talking and he is like "I don't want you to be friends with him I don't want you to talk to him' so I was like 'oh ya ok' I just lie to him oh well oh."
>
> Manal: When was that?
>
> Abby: Oh it was this year so I told him like oh ya cause I was telling him to leave me alone or something.
>
> Manal: So you lie to him?
>
> Abby: Yeah, cause then he gets all like nosey. He doesn't understand he just doesn't he is just like that.
>
> Manal: What about your mom don't you negotiate with her?
>
> Abby: My mother doesn't care it is whatever my father says goes because she doesn't want to get in fights and stuff.
>
> Manal: So do you think your mother thinks differently than your father?
>
> Abby: Nooooo.
>
> Manal: How do you feel about your father restricting you?
>
> Abby: I am fine for now because he does not know. I don't have to tell him.
>
> Manal: Doesn't it make you uncomfortable to lie?
>
> Abby: Ummmmmmm, well like after school I can really stay till a certain time and then ah if he sees like that I am sitting with the guy and talking to him he is like (with a deep mocking voice) 'what were you doing and blablabla' I am like 'I was just talking'.
>
> Manal: Does it scare you when he talks to you like that?
>
> Abby: It annoys me, just annoying; it does not scare me, just annoying.
>
> Manal: But why don't you explain to him?
>
> Abby: Ha, I just lie I am like okay "well we are talking about class" or something. Right now if they don't know it is easier than explaining to them. I don't like talking to them.

Abby continued to show how she strategized to resist and deveil her father's ethical *hijab*. By figuring her father's reasoning and confronting him with bigger forbiddens she out smarted him and stopped him from coercing her not to befriend boys.

> Abby: I don't want my dad to know [or see her scrap book with her boyfriend in it]. He like would say "what is this that I hear about you liking guys." I say "what you want me to see girls?" (The girls laugh) I told him 'what do you want me to date girls' seriously 'what the hell do you want me to do to turn gay or something'?" (The girls laugh). He got over it. Well he never tells me about guys any more. Our parents think they are smart.

> Layla: They think they are smarter than us, yeah they are not.

Amy on the other hand, had less to share about how she strategized to uncover the *hijabs*. Her mother gave her more leeway and allowed her to befriend boys as long as she met them and communicated with their mothers too. Yet, when it was time for the homecoming football game, the first for Amy since she just became a freshman, she asked me to escort her so her mom would allow her to go. Her mother was pleased that I could go with her because evening times were not suitable for her to leave the house and take Amy herself. At the football game, Amy introduced me to some of her friends. I asked Amy to stay within sight and not to do anything her mom would not approve. Based on what Amy shared with me in this occasion, Amy's mother did not know anything about this boy friend. On the way home, I discussed with Amy the importance of keeping her mother's trust and friendship by sharing with her what she experienced that day. Amy assured me that she is open with her mother and that she is a very understanding mother. Again, in this short excursion, Amy figured she could uncover and negotiate her own meaning of the spatial and ethical *hijab* in my company, away from her mother—at least once or until she shares it with her mother in the way and time, she chooses.

(Re)Narrating *muslim* Girls: "Like There Is an Infinite Way to Describe Us, Like it Doesn't Stop"

Layla, Dojua, Abby and Amy crossed the fourth spiritual *hijab* in spaces and moments outside the reach of the *hijab* discourse. During the second third of the study, the girls worked on a visual art project of two parts, (1) a group body collage, and (2) individual scrapbooks. The idea of making this project came up while the girls were discussing self-taken photos and magazine images they cut as part of a self-mapping task. This was a pre-designed task that I hoped would help inspire more body stories out of the girls' daily lives in different places and with different people (Oliver, 2003).

Layla, Dojua, Abby, and Amy decided to create the body collage and the scrapbooks as appropriate media to represent themselves to other teachers. First, this was their suggestion on how to help me achieve the purpose of this study and disseminate its outcomes. Earlier, I explained to them that I was interested in learning with/from them about their bodily experiences then presenting what we learn together to other teachers who work with Muslim girls. Right from the beginning of the design phase of this project, the girls named the body collage, the *InFinite Us*.

Layla explained, "Like there is an infinite way to describe us like it doesn't stop."

We all went together to an art material shop in town and the girls chose what they liked and what they needed to make the body collage and the scrap books. They bought banner paper for the collage and colored paper for scrapbooks. As soon as the idea of making a collective collage was first suggested by Dojua, the other girls liked it as well and started a collective planning and creative process lasting seven meetings.

> Dojua: I got a better idea we draw our body and we decorate parts of our bodies of ourselves and all around the thing we put our pictures. Yeah.
>
> Abby: Yeah, I get it, it is wild.
>
> Dojua: Decorate inside the body with pencils and stuff and we can like write and stuff like "passion" or whatever and outside we put our pictures.
>
> Abby: That makes sense.
>
> Dojua: Arms of Layla, my shoulders and my hairs. (Giggles)

The girls debated how to design the body collage and Dojua was leading. She said giggling, "We make one deformed body, one arm long and one short." They all agreed and started to improvise. They put down the banner paper on the floor and drew a body silhouette marking the borders of their body parts. With the music on and having fun, they were taking turns lying on the paper and marking the borders of Dojua's head and shoulders, Abby's torso and hips, Layla's right arm and left leg, and Amy's left arm and right leg.

Collectively, the girls decided on the content of the collage. They filled the outside of the body with photos I took of them making the collage in the study lounge and working out in the gym. They also used images they downloaded from the Internet such as photos of clouds, flowers, and running shoes. These images were black and white printed on regular paper, cut, and glued irregularly around the body. Inside the body silhouette, they pasted self-selected Internet and magazine clippings of words, quotes, music and movie stars' images, fashion images such as shoes, hair, watches, and underwear. This content represented their interests in socializing and dressing as well as their dreams of who they would like to be and how they would like to be read and learned by others. For example, the hair and the legs of the big body silhouette were made of many different textures, colors, and styles. Dojua explained this by saying,

> Ummmm the hair (laughs) we put together, we are kind of out all kinds of different things, like hair colors and textures like explaining us because there are so many different ways that define us.

Additionally, Abby suggested adding the words to the images and the textures because, "I like words." They distributed the words on the body parts (Appendix G). For example, the girls glued the following words, "hip hop, AT THE DISCO," "rap," "classical rock," "ROCK STAR, DEF LEPPARD" repeated and spread allover the body collage. Throughout their work in the study lounge, they downloaded free music from the Internet and they exchanged burned CD every time we met.

Close to the end of the study and as the girls' conversations around the design and the content of the collage and the scrapbooks was evolving, they thought that presenting the outcome of this project to my advisor, Dr. Kim Oliver, would help them practice expressing what and who they are to any outsider and more importantly to their teachers.

> Layla said: We can tell the people how we think.
>
> Dojua confirmed: Like there are other ways we think.
>
> Amy explained further: So people would know more about us.
>
> Abby added: Because not everybody understands how much time it takes to get to know us, they just need to listen more … so [teachers] would know who we are and what we are so they teach us better.
>
> Layla followed: So you [teachers] appreciate us more … and can make more activities for girls our age.
>
> Dojua added: I want teachers to know that I am a teenage girl; I am just like any other girl.

For almost 2 hours on the last formal day in the study, the girls took turns in narrating the *InFinite Us* body collage and their scrapbooks to Kim. They started all in one voice shouting the title of the body collage and the purpose of the presentation. They said:

> It is the *InFinite Us*. It is "What we are like."

This presentation was a dialogical conversation in which the girls talked about the images, the quotes, and the shapes in the collage and the scrapbooks as well as answered Kim's interjecting questions. This conversation elucidated the girls' multiplicities in their way of dress, socializing, dreaming of their futures, and, not surprisingly, their similarities to other girls their age in the public schools of the United States. They wanted to show outsiders to the Muslim community that they are not all the same though they are Muslim.

Amy confirmed: We are all different.

Abby added: Even though we are the same religion.

Layla interrupted her and said: We are the same, but people categorize us as the same because of religion or race but we are all so different.

The girls tried to explain themselves to Kim and to counter the prevailing representations of Muslims in the United States at the time.

Amy said: It wasn't like that before though … before 9/11.

Abby said: They just listen to the statistics in the media.

Layla added: Yeah, they all have a mind set on how Muslims are.

Amy continued: Yeah, we are all not the same [because] usually they look at us like well sometimes they don't know.

Dojua then said: Before 9/11 when people were asking me what I originally was. I said Muslim, and they really did not know what it was.

Abby said: People have stereotypes out there. They just listen to statistics on TV and stuff. We are doing this to eliminate this sort of stereotyping or that statistics are not the only thing.

Expressing how they are similar to other girls their age, Layla, who acted often as the lead DJ during our time together in the study lounge or in the car, said, "It feels weird without music in here, music is our life" and Dojua backed her up, "We cannot focus without music, music cleans my head." When they started the presentation to Kim with their favorite song, Layla said, "Music is part of us so we start [the presentation] with it." They further expressed in presenting the body collage what hip-hop meant to them and why they liked it.

Layla said: Like it is hard to explain like they're things come with hip hop like, you know what I mean?

Then Layla laughed and said: Oh, I like the music, styles, and the way of talking.

Abby added: The way of dressing.

Amy went on explaining: We are all of those different words.

And they read altogether in one loud voice: "HOT" goes with "MAN," "secrets," we have a lot of those, and 'terrorists' because people call us terrorists.

The final body collage itself became a big poster showing Layla, Dojua, Abby, and Amy as the *InFinite Us*. The girls were expressing themselves through their interests, fashion, music, and art, within the popular culture of their location. At the same time, they were expressing themselves so far away from any of the *hijabs* they faced in the other spaces and activities of the study. In other words, the name they selected for the collage and the content of the collage all represented the girls' multiplicities not only countering *hijabs* but also countering the prevailing post-9/11discourse about all Muslims.

Each scrapbook was made of a few pages from which each one of the girls chose the paper color. The girls decided to independently make individual scrapbooks as part of the artwork project and show the individuality of each one of them. For example, Amy said, "We are all really really different." One of the pages in Amy's book was titled "behind the scenes" and had an image of a boy with a clown face, and another was titled "changing faces" with photos of her with her many friends in school. On these two pages Amy explained, "You have to get to know him [the clown] just like me you need to get to know me."

The scrapbook became another private space each girl revealed more of her particularities, or more than she communicated at the beginning of the study through journaling for example. By playing with these images and through the time spent around each other creating these books, the girls expressed their complex selves much more in details more than with their written words in their private journals. Some common and important themes surfaced from making and presenting the scrapbooks, such as music and dancing, handsome boys, friends who Amy called "Homies," fashion and looking good. But each one of them highlighted in her book something more particular about herself. Layla for example who is more into hip-hop than other forms of music, said while giggling and explaining why she liked hip hop,

This is music and it is like my whole life ... that is a picture of me listening to music, that is a rapper, that's like my favorite all-girl band ... Charlotte Yates, I think like she is the best woman singer ever. She is going out with Jay Z, the biggest rapper ever. And that is Keyshia Cole, she is an R&B singer.... The words, you can dance to, like they aren't like they are rebels they are not stupid.

Dojua showed her passion for shopping especially shoes and Victoria Secret items. Rap music and rappers took one page of her scrapbook, and she said,

> Jay Z is one of the best rappers there is. I also like R & B cause it is not like hip hop like all of life is harsh and stuff it is about love.

Abby who likes "to laugh" had all sorts of jokes she picked up from different Internet sites. She is the joker in the group. A couple of the funny quotes she explained to Kim showed her sense of humor and her way of using words. She addressed Kim and said,

> You start tilting your head to smile :-) [giggling] Did you get it? ... cause to do a smiley face you have to do a semicolon like :.. here is another one, "If you were a booger, I'd pick you first!" [giggling]

Additionally, Abby showed her photography work that brought out her interest in befriending boys in sports and especially football. She also showed photos of some of the stars she watched on TV and some of the photos she took with her family in Hawaii in the summer. Finally, Amy read from the first page of her scrapbook emphasizing her love for music as well as her hybridity,

> "My WORLD" where she pasted numerous photos with her best friend, with a smaller letter clipping of sole sisters ... Music is me ... this says "New York, New York" because I am from New York ... I moved here when I was in fourth grade.

Within the content material, that is, photos, images, words, and quotes, within the body collage and scrapbooks, the collective stories of the girls told what they liked from music to food, to boys, to sports, and to fashion. Within the content of the scrapbooks, the singular stories of each of the girls were also expressed.

The girls creating the artwork and presenting it as their complex stories enabled them to renarrate their multiple selves outside the *hijab* discourse altogether. They experienced themselves doing something they chose to do. They created it outside the experiences of having to negotiate the *hijab* discourse. Layla, Dojua, Abby, and Amy were in a space that brought out their voices and honored them too. The girls heard themselves speak out their interests and desires from friends, to music, and to fashion without battling with the *hijab* discourse.

I listened to these girls rehearsing the presentation and encouraged them to say whatever they liked. When Kim listened to them too, they had another chance to express more of themselves without fears of reduction to a sexualized body or a passive helpless girl. In making the collage and the scrapbook and the collage, the girls briefly expressed how each one of them could be a *new* Muslim girl and different than the one whom started the study (Greene, 1995). To their surprise, the body collage and the scrapbooks showed how different they were from each other as well as how particular each one of them is. In this project, Layla, Dojua, Abby, and Amy were in another world expressing themselves without anyone shadowing them and without any *hijabs* at all.

In this process of making the artwork and presenting it to Kim, the girls were learning and playing freely without putting any energy into the negotiation of the *hijab*. They were in a space of safety in which others were carefully listening to them and acknowledging their many interests. Through living this visual creative process, a space of possibilities, the girls expressed themselves through another discourse. This self-suggested and self-directed creative project also was an opportunity for the girls to discover themselves in the friendships they cultivated and recognized they needed beyond the time of the study. Layla said, "we thought like we didn't have this much difference between us, we are really different but we all face the same pressure ... we trust each other more too."

SUMMARY

In this chapter, I discussed how three *hijabs*—visual, spatial and ethical— acted as a central gendering discourse in the lives of Layla, Dojua, Abby, and Amy, the four Muslim girls who participated in the study. At the beginning of the study, the girls seemed to be restricted by their parents' interpretations of three *hijabs*, in their dress, social activities and physical activities, and movement in public. However, as they participated in more of the interactive methods in the study and in various physical activities, they questioned their parents' diverse *hijabs* and finally deveiled them using several strategies to cross the fourth spiritual *hijab*. In spaces and moments outside the reach of the *hijab* discourse, the girls directed a creative project that allowed them to learn about themselves and build solidarity among themselves. In this opportunity, they renarrated their hybridity as Muslim girls and they called for teachers to pay attention to them with their differences, and, with their commonalities with other girls their age living in U.S. public schools.

What follows is discussion of the implications of this study leading to my vision of *deveiling* pedagogies.

CHAPTER 6

A VISION OF *DEVEILING* PEDAGOGIES

Because not everybody understands how much time it takes to get to know us, they [teachers] just need to listen more ... so they appreciate us more and make more activities for girls like us ... so they would know who we are and what we are so they teach us better. (Abby)

So you [teachers] appreciate us more ... and can make more activities for girls our age. (Layla)

I want teachers to know that I am a teenage girl; I am just like any other girl. (Dojua)

In this final chapter, I present the implications of this study leading to a vision of *deveiling* pedagogies. First, I present the implications of, using feminist *ijtihad*, negotiating differences in the process of gaining access (made possible by using my insider's literacies, my fluid insiderness, and building and maintaining relationships with key participants) in the lives of the four Muslim girls, and practicing agency to counter the *hijab* discourse. Finally, I share my vision for pedagogies of *deveiling* with those who are interested in working *with/among muslim* girls and their parents. I offer this vision to those who are committed to creating antiracist, anticolonial, antioppressive, and critical multicultural research and educational opportunities.

In this vision of *deveiling* pedagogies and research approaches, I imagine how feminist *ijtihad* needs to be an integral part of curriculum and an accessible tool of inquiry for *muslim* students. I imagine the use of

Pedagogies of Deveiling: Muslim Girls and the Hijab Discourse,
pp. 113–131

insider's literacies with creative methods to help in recognizing and negotiating the difference between educators and *muslim* girls' parents. I imagine educators collaborating with *muslim* girls to open possibilities for questioning hegemonies and practice agency to counter any normative discourses in their lives, including the *hijab* discourse.

This is a vision of *deveiling* pedagogies and research that was first inspired by the works of postcolonial feminist scholars like Sara Ahmed (2002), Nina Asher (2007), Meetoo and Mirza (2007), and Sherene Razack (2008). It was inspired by their calls to problematize the studies about/on *muslim* youth by exposing the array of racializing and ethnicizing discourses, which *muslims* have to constantly negotiate in transnational and diasporic contexts. A vision of *deveiling* pedagogies and research was particularly inspired specifically by their calls to recognize the intersecting discourses of colonialism, racism, and Islamophobia in the nation and sexism in *muslim* communities, that *muslimat* have to negotiate constantly (Ahmed, 2002; Zine, 2006a, 2006b). It was a response to their calls to counter "the culturalization of racism" (Razack, 2008, p. 171) that is increasing in academic research done on/about *muslim* females.

IMPLICATIONS OF *DEVEILING*

Using Feminist *Ijtihad*

> So let us raise the sails and lift the veils—the sails of memory-ship. But first let us lift the veils with which our contemporaries disguise the past in order to dim our present. (Mernissi, 1991, p. ii)

This first implication of this study arises from doing feminist *ijtihad*. It is my expansion on the *deveiling* research of *arab-muslim* feminists; specifically Fatima Mernissi's (1991) that helped conceptualize this study (Chapter 2). This is the kind of *ijtihad* that made it possible to expose how controlling access to the interpretation of the sacred texts, Qur'an and the Hadīth, and popularizing the androcentric meanings of the *hijabs*, had enabled a gendering discourse central to the lives of Muslim women. My use of *ijtihad* made it possible to access the insider's classical Islamic tools of interpretations (*tafsir*), such as of *asbab al nuzul, isnad,* and *matn.* This *ijtihad* exposed the multiplicity and fluidity of the first three *hijabs*—visual, spatial, and ethical. More importantly, it is the kind of *ijtihad* that made it possible to expose the potential of the fourth *hijab*—spiritual—that urges Muslims to pursue deeper knowledge. It exposed how crossing the spiritual *hijab* or the virtue of pursing deeper knowledge has been censored, and thus, the possibilities of acknowledging the *hijab* discourse have been disguised. Thus, using feminist *ijtihad* demystified the tasks of researching and interpreting the Qur'an and the Hadīth and illustrated its accessibility to all Muslim without a mediator.

In doing feminist *ijtihad*, I exposed how the control of language and the interpretation of all 16 *hijab*-related Qur'anic verses and a major misogynistic *hadīth* enabled the *hijab* discourse. I expanded on Mernissi's deconstructive analysis of the four *hijabs*—visible, spatial, ethical, and spiritual—in the canonical texts of *Lisan Al 'Arab*, the Qur'an and the Hadīth (Chapter 2). In this, I illustrated how feminist *ijtihad* deveiled the *hijabs* that were socially constructed as a gendering discourse in the lives of *muslimat*. Using the same classical Islamic research tools monopolized by the androcentric interpreters of the sacred Qur'anic and the Hadīth text (Clarke, 2003; Kugle, 2010; Mernissi, 1991; Wadud, 1999), I highlighted three steps Mernissi used to deveil the *hijabs*. I showed how by, (1) doing a philological analysis, (2) contextualizing the Qur'anic *hijab* verses, and (3) deauthenticating popular misogynist *ahadīth*, the first three *hijabs* enabled a gendering discourse hegemonizing Muslim women's bodies in dress, behavior, and presence in public.

The first *deveiling* step, doing a philological analysis, expanded the *hijabs'* reduced linguistic scope. It was a step of *deveiling* the four dimensions of the *hijab* from the visible two popularized physically marked representations—visual and spatial—to the invisible and subtle third and fourth—the ethical and the spiritual. By expanding the meaning of the *hijab* from the superficialized visual representation of a headscarf to the more complex and interwoven spatial and ethical *hijabs*, this step of *deveiling* illustrated how the social complex codes of a gendering discourse were constructed. But more importantly, this step opened the potential of the *hijab* as a notion of multiple and shifting meanings, and at the same time, as a barrier that may be crossed in pursuit of deeper knowledge.

With the potential of the expanded meanings of the *hijabs*, the second *deveiling* step became possible. The step of contextualizing all the relevant *hijab* Qur'anic verses (total 16) and not only the three verses that are most misinterpreted and most popular (33:53; 33:59; 24:31). First, when contextualized, the term *hijab* in the most popular Qur'anic verse (33:53) did not mean the spatial separation between men and women or the seclusion of Muslim women from public lives. Rather, it meant the circumstantial separation between the Prophet and his male guests. Second, when interpreted out of history, the *hijab*-related term, *jalābībihinna*, in another very popular Qur'anic verse (33:59), went beyond the meaning of a specific cloak to distinguish the Prophet's wives throughout His lifetime. When contextualized and historicized, this *hijab* was clearly not meant to be generalized on all Muslim women at all times nor was it a pure Islamic practice. Ahmed (1992) explains,

> The phrase "[she] took the veil" is used in the hadith to mean that a woman became a wife of Muhammad's suggests that for some time after Muhammad's death, when the material incorporated into the hadith was circulated, veiling and seclusion were still considered peculiar to Muhammad's wives. It is not known how the customs spread to the rest of the community. The Muslim conquests of areas which veiling was commonplace among the upper classes, the influx of wealth, the resultant raised status of Arabs, and Muhammad's wives being take as models probably combined to bring about their general adoption. (pp. 55-56)

Moreover, when verse (24:31) is read in combination with verse (24:30), the visual and the ethical *hijabs* did not only mean covering women's bodies. The *hijabs* rather meant that modesty in dress and behavior are obligatory for both Muslim men and women. By exposing the decontextualized interpretations of the three main *hijab* verses (33:53; 33:59; 24:31), I highlighted how these verses have been used as the unquestionable conduit to the hegemonizing effects of the visual and spatial *hijabs*, and thus, generalized to all Muslim women at all times.

Moreover, given that the spiritual *hijab* appears in 10 out of the total 16 *hijab* verses (7:46; 17:45; 38:32; 41:5; 42:51; 83:15; 6:25; 12:107; 18:57; and 50:22) and it refers to the barrier that excludes the believers from the spiritual privileges of knowing Allah and the Prophet's message (Mernissi, 1991), it should be the most pursued by all Muslims. However, the visual and spatial meanings of the *hijab* were overgeneralized to all times and to all Muslim women and were emphasized and prioritized over the more called for spiritual *hijab*, which was conveniently displaced outside the lived experiences of all Muslims.

The *deveiling* of the decontextualized interpretations of the 16 Qura'nic verses illustrated how the *hijab* was reduced to its visual and spatial physical meanings obscuring a main message of Islam, the pursuit of deeper knowledge and spiritual grace of being a Muslim. This *deveiling* step showed that the emphasis of the majority of the *hijab* terms that appear in 16 *hijab* related Qur'anic verses are not about the segregation between men and women nor about the special dressing of women, but on the contrary, they are about a core call of the Qur'an for Muslims to pursue deeper knowledge.

The third *deveiling* step reexposed Mernissi's work of deauthenticating a major popular misogynistic *hadīth*. Due to the misogynist context in which the *falah hadīth* was first recalled, its recollection by an androcentric narrator, and its circulation as an authentic *hadīth* cited in the very credible source of Sahih Al Bukhari, women were easily constructed as the instigators of affliction and strife amongst Muslims, and thus, unworthy of leading in the public realm. This *deveiling* step showed that the construction of women as sources of danger objectified them and in return helped support the justification to hegemonize the visual and spatial *hijabs* in the lives of Muslim women.

The three *deveiling* steps of feminist *ijtihad*, using insider's Islamic classical tools, illustrated how the interpretation of the sacred text may be open to all Muslims, including myself—a researcher and educator committed to social justice and equity. That is, using these tools to deveil the sources of interpretations and the resulting hegemonized meanings, and thus, pursue deeper knowledge is the responsibility of all Muslims. The use of these tools is the right of every Muslim and not only a few elite male androcentric scholars. Open access of using interpretative tools brings the possibilities for researchers and educators to collaborate with Muslim students and their parents and make sense of their *muslimness* directly in relation to the sacred text. It brings the possibilities of applying the classical Islamic tools of interpretations to the lives of Muslim youth living several normative discourses at this time.

This kind of feminist *ijtihad* is committed to exposing how androcentric Islamic authorities forbade common Muslims especially those from the margins of the community like women, young people, "people from sexual and gender minorities" (Kugle, 2010, p. 40), to engage in any Qur'anic interpretation. That is, these common and marginalized Muslims were kept ignorant from using the tools of *ijtihad* and denied the "very right to interact directly and personally with the Qur'an" (Kugle, 2010, p. 40). As such, Muslims were forbidden from questioning the popularized and unjust interpretations of the Qur'an and are conveniently restricted from pursuing deeper spiritual and religious knowledge inclusive of all of them in their varieties across the globe. Keeping the interpretations of the Qur'an and the tools of *ijtihad* in the hands of a few powerful elite confines the common Muslim to ignorance of the possibilities of making sense of their world and changing the inequities and injustices they face in it. This state of ignorance is in contradiction with the first call in the Qur'an (96:1-4) with which Allah ordered Muslims to read, reread, and pursue deeper knowledge.

اقْرَأْ بِاسْمِ رَبِّكَ الَّذِي خَلَقَ. خَلَقَ الإِنسَانَ مِنْ عَلَقٍ. اقْرَأْ وَرَبُّكَ الأَكْرَمُ. الَّذِي عَلَّمَ بِالْقَلَمِ. (القرآن الكريم، ٩٦: ١-٤)

Read in the name of your Lord Who created. He created human from a clot. Read and your Lord is Most Honorable. He Who taught (the use of) the pen. (The Qur'an, 96:1-4)

That is, to interrupt this state of ignorance, Kugle calls for progressive *ijtihad,* "struggle with words" (2010, p. 43) or the need to reinterpret the Qur'an with a commitment to love and justice. This the invitation of Allah in the following verse,

ادْعُ إِلَى سَبِيلِ رَبِّكَ بِالْحِكْمَةِ وَالْمَوْعِظَةِ الْحَسَنَةِ وَجَادِلْهُم بِالَّتِي هِيَ أَحْسَنُ إِنَّ رَبَّكَ هُوَ أَعْلَمُ بِمَن ضَلَّ عَن سَبِيلِهِ وَهُوَ أَعْلَمُ بِالْمُهْتَدِينَ. (القرآن الكريم، ١٦:١٢٥)

Invite (all) to the Way of your Lord with wisdom and beautiful counsel; and argue with them in ways that are best and most gracious, for thy Lord knoweth best, who have strayed from His Path, and who receive guidance. (The Qur'an, 16:125)

This kind of feminist *ijtihad* also illustrated that exposing the *hijab's* multiple, shifting, and deferred meanings, opened the possibilities of revealing *its* fragility, contradictions, and thus, the (im)possibilities of an ever-lasting gendering discourse (Gannon & Davies, 2007). With this exposure, comes a potential for critiquing the androcentric interpretations of the text or enabling the reinterpretations of the multiple and fluid values and practices of the *hijabs*. This move enables the destabilization of any of the *hijabs* discursive hegemonizing consequences. This kind of feminist *ijtihad* opens a wide field for a range of multiple and simultaneous readings of the *hijab* that researchers and educators need to consider any time they are working with/among *muslim* youth. This kind of feminist *ijtihad* is a basis for a curriculum of critical inquiry that should be accessible to *muslim* youth. This is a *deveiling* pedagogy that makes insider's Islamic tools of research accessible to young *muslims*, and thus, possible to practice without mediators. Feminist *ijtihad* is a *deveiling* curriculum that cultivates *muslim* youth's skills and language and enables them to become producers of knowledge and active agents in their own lives.

Negotiating Differences in the Process of Gaining Access

The development of the individual, personal, intimate relationships between researchers and participants rests on and contains an implicit contract, the terms of which are difficult to foresee or make explicit and the arena for differing assumptions, expectations, and contingencies. (Josselson, 2007, p. 539)

The second implication of this study arises from the complexities facing researchers in the process of gaining entry and maintaining access into the lives of *muslim* girls (Chapter 4). Differences of positionalities over my *muslimness*, the subtle diversity of the interpretations of the first three *hijabs*, and thus the *hijab* discourse itself between the girls' parents and myself, all emerged as major challenges to access.

By using feminist *ijtihad* and my insider's literacies of the Qur'an, Arabic, history of Islam, the *hijabs*, and history and politics of the parents' countries of birth, I was able to recognize and negotiate these differences throughout the study. One, doing feminist *ijtihad* enabled me to recognize the *hijabs* and the *hijab* discourse itself as central in the lives of *muslims* and as a marker of difference with the parents. It also allowed me to recognize the vulnerabilities of the *hijabs'* interpretations, and thus, the negotiability of the discourse itself.

Two, as the main researcher in this study identifying as *arabyyah-muslimah*, on the one hand, I was positioned as an outsider in this study (Hill-Collins 1990). My seemingly nonobservance of the daily prayers and fasting Ramadan, nonembodiment of the visible *hijabs*, and academic status all positioned me as an outsider. On the other hand, I was distinctly an insider with my Arabic-Muslim name and with my insider's literacies (Anzaldúa, 1987; Mohanty, 2003). I am multilingual. Arabic is my *home* language and Islam is my religion by birth. I was schooled in Jordan and have spent 17 years of my life working mainly in Jordan and Palestine. Most of my life, I have lived in Arab-Muslim contexts in which I had to constantly negotiate the *hijab* discourse complicated by my gender, class, education, sexuality, physical ability, citizenship, geographical location, and ways of thinking and doing my *muslimness* (Swarr & Ngar, 2010). With these insider's positionalities, I have gained literacies of Arabic, contemporary Arab politics, Islamic and Arab histories, and Islam's fundamental texts.

Using my insider's literacies and the persistant practice of "strong reflexivity" (Hesse-Biber & Leavy, 2007, p. 15), I was able to stay mindful of the differences with any of the participants in the project and more diligent in negotiating them throughout the research process (Hesse-Biber & Leavy, 2007). That is, I was more aware and open to negotiate the challenges of any emerging difference within this study between myself and the girls' parents. Using my insider's literacies and critical reflexivity I was able to read the subtle diversity of the parents' interpretations of the first three *hijabs*, and thus, the recognition of openings to negotiate differences with them over the *hijab* discourse. My insider's literacies also enabled me to recognize the differences of my *muslimness* with the parents. Recognizing the subtleties and the overlapping of these differences and negotiating them, were crucial in balancing and maintaining the trust of seven parents. As a result, I was able to maintain access to the girls' time, and assure their participation throughout the study.

My name and country of birth helped me enter the women's quarters in one of the local the mosques, the first site of the study, the only meeting space the Muslim girls in town had outside school. However, after spending some time at the mosque, it became clear that it was offering the girls limited activities to enjoy, little privacy, and little time to spend together and with me every week. As an insider speaking Arabic with the head of the board of the mosque, the teachers, and the mothers, I was able to read the nuances of these conditions and realize that they would not be helpful in building trust relationships with me and solidarity together, and thus, would not serve the purpose of the study. Thus, after spending a few weeks in the mosque I decided to find a more appropriate site for the study. I used my insider's literacies to negotiate the three *hijabs*—visual, spatial and ethical—with the mothers approving the activity center as the site for the study.

With my position at the university in town and my advisor's departmental base, I was able to provide the activity center on campus as an alternative site for the study. To move out of the mosque to a new site and guarantee the approval of the parents, I invited the mothers for a visit to the activity center. They were impressed with the possibilities of activities that would be available not only to teach their daughters new physical activities but also to "fill their time" with something beneficial and entertaining during their summer vacation. Moving the study site to the university's activity center did not minimize differences over the *hijab* discourse with the teachers and the parents. Rather, these differences became more explicit and confined between the parents and myself. As a result, negotiating these differences in this site maximized the range of activities the girls were able to practice as well as extended the time I spent with them.

With my insider's literacies, I recognized the subtle differences with the parents over my *muslimness*, that is, my submission to the will of Allah, adherence to the daily prayers, and fasting Ramadan. First, I recognized the difference over the parents' submission to the will of Allah with their frequent utterance of *inshallah*—God willing. Though this momentarily seemed that the parents disproved an activity, it did not reflect their final unwillingness to have me continue working with their daughters. That is, the difference over our *muslimness* was negotiable and the parents' approval of the activities presented to the girls every week we met was possible. Second, my modesty and the *harams* emerged more as the markers of difference over the multiple interpretations of the *hijabs*, and thus, the *hijab* discourse itself. This was more of a serious challenge to my eligibility to gain entry and the legitimacy of the activities in the study. However, with my ability to speak Arabic, to recite verbatim Qur'anic verses, and reiterate Mohammed's teachings when an opportunity rose in my conversations with the parents or with the head of the mosque's board, I was able to negotiate the extent of my modesty in dress or behavior as satisfactory and the range of spaces and activities as not *haram*, and thus, suitable to use in the study.

Recognizing and negotiating differences between the parents and myself, thus gaining entry into the spaces and activities and maintaining the participation of four Muslim girls in the study, was directly dependent on maintaining trust relationships with the girls' parents—Malikah, Khatimah, Zeena, Jamilah, Iyad, Samer, and Ghazi (A.S.M. Hamzeh, 2007). Though seven of the parents were secondary participants in this study, maintaining relationships with them was a challenging process that took a great deal of time and communication and it was tested almost at every contact I had with each of them. I had to listen to the mothers subtle interpretations of the *hijabs* in relation to the weekly activities the girls choose and negotiate our differences over hours of conversations before and after the Saturday meetings with the girls. In order to maintain the four major parental relationships in the last 6 months of the study, I had to go to several of the parents' homes and work places beyond the formal sites of the study. I also had to spend time socializing separately with four of the mothers and two fathers almost every week. This was beyond the 170 hours I spent with the four girls. Each time I encountered one of the parents; I had to negotiate our differences on one or more of the *hijabs*. Additionally, I engaged with each of the parents in their homes or at the doorsteps every week when I picked up or dropped off their daughters. These were moments when I used "reflexive interplay" and became more aware of the emerging differences with the parents over the *hijab* discourse. I took the opportunity to mediate these differences and make "meaning of questions that are asked and how those questions are answered and interpreted" (Hesse-Biber & Piatelli, 2007, p. 500). That is, I tried to find a common ground to address the parents' concerns about any of the study's activities and negotiate a way to maintain access into the lives of their daughters.

At the same time, I was sharing with the parents some of what I learned about the girls that would benefit their relationships with their daughters. All of them expressed their appreciation of the benefits their daughters were gaining by participating in this study. Sharing with the mothers a common interest, their daughters' well being, helped strengthen my relationship with them. The long conversations with the parents were essential to reflect my respect to their readings of the *hijabs* and to find ways to work our differences. With every contact with the seven parents—six mothers, and three fathers—I had to balance my insider's literacies with their respectability, and thus, assure entry and access in this study. Thus, my commitment to maintaining strong relationships with the girls' parents became central to the success of access in this study.

Though, three of the fathers in this study signed the consent forms, the mothers were more in charge of granting the rest of the permissions throughout the study. That is, I have to underscore the obvious, that the entry in this study would have been almost impossible if I was not female and without having a great deal of contact with the four mothers in this study. This is to emphasize that the process of gaining entry in the lives of *muslim* girls need to be taken seriously especially for those researchers and teachers with little or no insider's literacies and who are not identified as females.

Access to the lives of Layla, Dojua, Abby, and Amy was an ongoing process (Clandinin, 2007; Lieblich, 2006; Subedi & Daza, 2008) both at the introduction of the study, explaining the purpose and methods, requesting signatures of the consent forms, as well as throughout, getting approval for every one of the 17 meetings I had with the girls. This study was a negotiation-driven process that allowed me to maintain access to the main site and the activities of the study, as well as maintaining my relationships with the mothers and the fathers of Layla, Dojua, Abby, and Amy. When this study started, I did not have an assured entry after a single event, like the signature on the consent form. The entry was a gradual and simultaneously a circular process that did not get me at one point "any approximation to total access" (Maxwell, 1996, p. 66). It was a process that required continuous reflexive thought and creative action (Clandinin, 2007; Maxwell, 1996). I did not start making contact with all of the final participants in one place or at one meeting. I did not obtain the final commitments to the study from all parents at one time. Additionally, the signed consent forms were not open-ended permissions to all the activities I planned for the girls. The complexity and uniqueness of gaining entry to this study shaped, (1) the accessibility of settings thus the range in the activities and the locations of the study and (2) the availability of the participants' thus their number and their diversity.

Doing research and learning with/among *muslim* youth and their parents calls for doing all that it takes to recognize and negotiate difference especially over the *hijab* discourse. Using insider's methodological approaches brings us closer to the beginning of working with/among young *muslim*s to counter the unjust consequences of the *hijab* discourse or any other normative discourses in their lives. Conceptualizating the *hijab*s and using insider's literacies, I opened possibilities to uncover the very implicit differences with the parents, especially over the *hijab* discourse as a major challenge to gaining entry and maintaining access. Paying attention to hidden markers of difference over the *hijab* discourse, such as modesty and *harams*, and using Arabic (Urdu, Farsi or any other language

Muslim girls and their families use as a home language) and the Qur'an and the Hadīth opened the possibility of building relationships with the girls parents, as well as creating safe and inviting spaces and activities for the Muslim girls to explore themselves and their ways of learning. That is, using insider's methodologies opens the possibilities of interrupting "racial thinking" (Razack, 2008) in research that approaches access with "culturally responsive" tactics, and end up constructing Muslims as one homogenous group in the schools of North America, Europe, and Australia.

Learning that gaining research access into the lives of Muslim girls was not a seamless process and using insider's methodological approaches may be more helpful in encouraging more antiracializing educational research be done *with muslim* girls. That is, by not focusing on the headscarf and instead paying attention to the *hijab* discourse as a site of difference, researchers and educators may open the possibilities of negotiating access in the lives of *muslim* girls. This might open possibilities of doing research with the *muslim* girls themselves and bring more insight to how they negotiate the *hijab* discourse with their parents, with the larger Muslim community, as well as with other people in their lives. The challenge is to recognize and negotiate difference in order to theorize the complexities of *muslim* girls' experiences and "build coalitions and solidarities across borders" (Mohanty, 2003, p. 226). That is, researchers who want to work with/among *muslim* girls need to rethink access that is "largely dependent on relationships developed overtime and within the particularities of context" (Craig & Huber, 2007, p. 262). That is, access to such research is deeply dependent on negotiating difference and building relationships and collaborations with the adults in the lives of the *muslim* girls. As such, researchers or educators, have to be in an ongoing reflexive mode and refuse to be situated outside the life process of the girls they are working *with*. They cannot assume automatic access to the lives of *muslim* girls. Researchers and educators need to be very cognizant that accessing the lives and learning trajectories of *muslim* girls is not an immediate or a neutral process (in Brown & Strega, 2005) but a collaborative and emergent process (Clandinin, 2007) that calls for the engagement and negotiation in any emerging difference between the participants and the researchers/educators.

Doing research and learning with/among *muslim* youth and their parents is a relationship that requires the use of feminist *ijtihad* and insider's literacies. Doing such research and pedagogy enables the researchers to recognize and negotiate the frequently overlooked differences of positionalities between the researchers and the participants (Fine, 2007; Lather, 2007; Reay, 2007)—especially over the *hijab* discourse. This the *deveiling* research and pedagogy that I see will make collaboration with *muslim* youth possible. This is the kind of *deveiling* research and pedagogy in which researchers and educators are willing to engage with any emerging differences with adults in their lives. I see that this is the kind of research and pedagogy that will open the chance to gain deeper insights on how to counter the unjust consequences of the *hijab* discourse, and of course, other normative discourses in the lives of young *muslim*s.

Practicing Agency to Counter the *Hijab* Discourse

> When I jumped in the pool fully clothed, [it] was something I will never forget. (Layla)

This third implication that rises from this study is the lesson of how Layla, Dojua, Abby, and Amy explored their extraordinary capacities for practicing their agency by negotiating the first three *Hijabs* and crossing the fourth (Chapter 5). Layla, Dojua, Abby, and Amy negotiated the *hijab* discourse by temporarily conforming to their parents' three *hijabs* or veils—the visual, spatial, and ethical. But more importantly, they used the opportunities presented to them in this study, to question these *hijabs* and strategized to uncover, deveil them. In other words, they practiced their agency to question, dissent, demand, and finally—even for short moments— experience "what could be" (Fine, 2007, p. 613). That is, the stories in this study confirm that the *hijab* discourse was central in the lives of Layla, Dojua, Abby, and Amy lives, but at the same they illustrate how it was possible for the girls to question the *hijabs* and to cross this central gendering discourse. Their questioning and negotiating the *hijabs*, reflects how the girls deveiled the first three *hijabs* and the crossed the fourth. Given the potential of recognizing the fourth *hijab* and the potential of crossing it and using interactive and alternative methods (Fine & McClelland, 2007), the girls went beyond the taken-for-granted in their lives so far. That is, the girls found their own creative ways to cross the fourth *hijab*, uncovered alternative ways of learning their bodies, interrupted inequities in their lives (Zine, Taylor, & Davis, 2007). They began to practice their agency and to enact their *muslimness* in new ways.

Throughout the study, I was not only keeping an eye on the subtle emergence of the first three *hijabs*—visual, spatial, and ethical—comprising the *hijab* discourse, but I was also staying open to the girls' subtle ways of *deveiling* these *hijabs* and crossing the fourth *hijab*. At the beginning, I was able to recognize the hegemonizing effect of the *hijab* discourse or how the girls conformed to their parents' seemingly fixed interpretations of the physical *hijabs* in their dress, participation in social activities and physical activities, and movement in public. Almost daily, both the girls' mothers and fathers scrutinized and tried to enforce the girls' modesty in dressing, veiled-off several spaces and activities from the girls, and challenged their befriending boys particularly and socializing with girls who were not Muslim. As such, the three *hijabs* were overwhelmingly challenging to these girls' participation in activities such as swimming, making friends whether with boys or girls, having fun, and eventually knowing their bodies and making their own wise decisions about/for them. That is, the girls' participation in public activities was conditional, depending on how much an activity or a place had the potential to make the girls violate any of their parents' interpretations of the *hijabs*.

However, later in the study, the girls began to question their parents' interpretations of the *hijabs*. These questionings made it clear that the parents' interpretations were not about the homogenous meanings of the "veil or not to veil" but about the varied and negotiable interpretations of the *hijabs*. With the girls' questioning further, they were trying to make sense of their parents' reasoning behind every *hijab* to which they asked them to comply. However, once the girls participated in all the activities presented to them; they made independent decisions choosing enjoyable physical activities that reflected their own multiple interpretations of the *hijabs*. They extended their invitation to the boys to play with them, took up swimming only in the last five meetings, and dressed up at the pool or on the basketball court in their own ways of being modest. In other words, when Layla, Dojua, Abby, and Amy had the lead and the opportunity to practice their own judgment and chose what they enjoyed from the physical activities offered in the study, they simply became active. By not stopping at critiquing their parents' interpretation of the three *hijabs* the girls found themselves resisting the first three *hijabs* altogether.

As the study progressed, the girls were seemingly still conforming to their parents' *hijabs* but they were actually beginning to resist them as well. They began to cross the *hijabs* first, by taking advantage of any minor privilege their parents allowed them in order to participate in public activities such as an adult escort, and/or, second, by using the study time to question and make more sense of these *hijabs*. With the weekly access to an independent time without the parents' direct monitoring yet with an adult escort, the girls began to discuss and question the *hijabs* that were obviously occupying their minds daily and dominating their lives. The safe spaces that became available in the study such as private journaling, small group discussions, and e-mails with me, presented the girls with opportunities to vent about the challenges of the *hijabs* and ask each other and myself questions about the *hijabs*' meanings and relevance to the context in which they live. Moreover, they questioned their fathers' reasoning and gender positions on the *hijabs*. Accordingly, the girls seemed to be struggling with the contradictions between their fathers' sexualizing stands on the *hijabs* and their own desires to participate in any learning opportunities presented to them in their daily lives. A this point in the study, the girls began to bring out their own doubts about the inscribed meanings of the *hijabs*, as well as expose the *hijabs'* contractions with their desires to learn and their striving to experience gender equity. Within the spaces and activities this study provided, as well as the solidarity amongst them and the trusting relationship they maintained with me, the girls started to express their own interpretations of these *hijabs* especially those that prohibited them from swimming and befriending boys. Along this process of doubting and questioning, the girls began to open the possibility of *deveiling* the three main *hijabs* altogether and exploring ways of practicing and owning their agencies (Weedon, 1999).

Finally, when the girls were expressing their interests in a space encouraging their creativity, they began to cross the fourth spiritual *hijab* and to express themselves outside the reach of the *hijab* discourse. They expressed their multiple subjectivities—girls who are into hip hop, fashion, Black boys, basketball, jokes, photography et cetera—and made them visible in the new possibilities of the study (Harris, 2004). They produced a new knowledge about the Muslim girl to share with others (Weis & Fine, 2004). They renarrated their complex body stories and expressed their multiple selves as the *"InFinite Us*. It is 'What we are like.'" As such, they were not only expressing themselves outside the *hijab* discourse but also *deveiling* or countering the racializing representations of Muslim girls in educational research through their ways of dress, socializing, and dreaming of their futures. They expressed how they could remake themselves when they had the chance. They told teachers to pay attention to their differences—though they all consider themselves Muslim—and their similarities to other girls their age in the public schools of the United States.

The girls practicing agency and interrupting the *hijab* discourse was made possible by using hybrid unclassical methods that invite "the unspeakable to be voiced" (Sirin & Fine, 2008, p. 198). These methods helped me build trust relationships with the girls and helped them form solidarity among each other. These methods also opened spaces for data to emerge that would not have been possible with predesigned questionnaires or short interviews for example. The use of taking photos with disposable cameras, journaling and e-mailing, selecting enjoyable physical activities and creating the body collage and scrap book project all contributed in voicing out the unspeakable on the *hijabs*—negotiating then crossing them altogether. All these methods gave me the opportunity to hang out with the girls outside the activity center and to listen to the spontaneous conversations the girls had among themselves to speak about their parents' three *hijabs* enforced on them, question these *hijabs*, and negotiate them.

The girls recognized and explored the opportunities within the activities and the spaces of this study and strategized to negotiate the *hijab* discourse. The girls' *deveiling* of the *hijab* discourse was apparent in their awareness of when, where, and how to conform with, argue, and/or cross their parents' interpretations of the *hijabs*. They took the opportunities in the study to deveil the *hijabs* in two specific ways. One, though sometimes they showed conformity to the parents' *hijabs*, they chose other more appropriate times to confront them and argue an alternative interpretation of the *hijabs*. Two, anytime they were away from their parents' direct monitoring and in a safe learning space, they independently decided to question, uncover, reinterpret, cross, embody and perform the three *hijabs* in multiple and fluid ways. Particularly by swimming at the university pool, which became a main activity in the study, the girls crossed all of the three *hijabs* and swimming became a major activity they chose to enjoy. With no regrets and enjoyment, the girls creatively redesigned their not so modest swimming outfits, threw "the rules out the window" and lounged around where boys or men were present, and argued their parents' *hijabs* and bent them to befriend boys.

Eventually, the girls showed that the *hijabs* are "dramatic and contingent construction of meaning[s]" (Butler, 1990, p. 190). In the *deveiling* possibilities of this study, the girls troubled the *hijabs'* reiteration as the norm, and thus, even shortly were able to interrupt the normativity of a gendering discourse central in their lives. In this, not only did they question the three *hijab*—visual, spatial, and ethical—but they also negotiated its multiple and fluid discursive possibilities. As such, the girls deveiled the normativity of the three *hijabs*, exposed their multiplicity and fluidity, and opened the slippages within/of the *hijab* discourse itself. Arguably, the *hijabs'* fluidity worked in the lives of these girls as openings to challenge and topple the *hijab* discourse with its consequential injustices. The *hijabs* are not impossible to deveil and the *hijab* discourse is interruptible. Through their continuous *deveiling*, practicing their agency, the girls challenged the *hijab* discourse itself and as a result interrupted its normative consequences. This process of *deveiling* is the:

> Formulation of "mo(ve)ments" [that] brings together "movement" and "moment" to stress that opportunities for agency, for ways of moving into different discursive frameworks, open and close in unexpected and transitory spaces. We use "mo(ve)ment" also to signify the simultaneity of memory and movement in the methodology of collective biography through which we shift analysis of lived experience from individual biography toward collective readings of discursive regimes, and through which we aim to dislodge habitual ways of thinking. (Gannon & Davies, 2007, p. 101)

The implications of doing feminist *ijtihad*, recognizing and negotiating differences with parents and the girls' *deveiling* of the *hijab* discourse gave me the chance to rethink research and pedagogical approaches when collaborating with young *muslims*. With this, I began to imagine how a vision of *deveiling* pedagogies and research would look like.

A VISION OF *DEVEILING* PEDAGOGIES

In a vision of *deveiling* pedagogies, I imagine there would be more feminist researchers and educators using feminist *ijtihad* with/among young *muslim* youth especially girls. I foresee *deveiling* pedagogies where scholars and educators are committed to, (1) understanding how to access and collaborate with *muslim* girls as agents negotiating the implications of normative discourses on their bodily experiences, and (2) finding more participatory and critically reflexive methodologies in anticolonial education research that would open spaces for young *muslim* girls to practice their agency, change inequities and be more critically literate of their own contexts.

In a vision of *deveiling* pedagogies, I anticipate that the first three *hijabs*—visual, spatial, and ethical—are troubled and finally recognized as another normative discourse challenging *muslim* girls beside the array of colonizing, racializing, and gendering discourses targeting *muslim* bodies in the transnational and diasporic contexts (Asher, 2003; Fine, 2004; Oliver, Hamzeh, & McCaughtry, 2009; Hamzeh, 2011; Razack, 2008; Sirin & Fine, 2008; Zine, 2006a). In a vision of *deveiling* pedagogies and research, I foresee that the use of feminist *ijtihad* will trouble the desire for clarity or the fixation of the meaning of the *hijab*. I see teachers and scholars looking out for the possibilities and opening spaces for new and alternative meanings of the *hijabs*. As such, they challenge any foreclosures of rethinking the *hijabs* discursively. According to Lather (1986),

> Rather than resolution, our task is to live out the ambivalent limits research as we move towards something more productive of an enabling violation of its disciplining effects. Inhabiting the practices of its rearticulation ... we occupy the very space opened up by the (im)possibilities of ethnographic representation. (p. 541)

In this vision of *deveiling* pedagogies, researchers and educators are aware how the *hijabs* became a gendering discourse that rendered the *muslimah's* body a site of contestation and control for several intersecting patriarchal and colonizing hegemonies (Ahmed, 2002; Asher, 2007; Meetoo & Mirza, 2007; Mernissi, 1991; Razack, 2008). That is, they are committed to challenging the *hijab's* taken-for-granted meanings and exposing the *hijab* discourse as one of the more complex and consistently challenging discursive experiences *muslimat* encounter. They will acknowledge that the *hijab* discourse is more critical in their lives and experiences than the reactionary and distracting debates over the "to veil or not to veil." I see educators and scholars breaking the silence about a major unexposed gendering discourse and its hegemonizing consequences on girls' opportunities in every realm in their lives. As such, they will open the chances with young *muslim* girls and boys to use alternative pedagogical and research methodologies that have the potential to counter this *hijab* discourse along with other discourses racializing and gendering them especially in neocolonial and diasporic contexts. Finding potential practices and spaces of changing the *hijab* discourse's consequential inequities is our main commitment as scholars working towards antioppressive pedagogies. Thus, the *hijab* discourse needs to be recognized as another discourse that intersects with other ethnicizing and gendering discourses with which the neocolonialists as well as Islamists exclude Muslimat in transnational and diasporic contexts (Ahmed, 2002; Razack, 2005).

In a vision of *deveiling* pedagogies and research, I imagine scholars and teachers in a vision of *deveiling* pedagogies research will be more dedicated to interrogating the multiple discourses—including the *hijab* discourse—constituting the complex bodily experiences of *muslim* girls especially those living in transnational and diasporic educational contexts (Subedi & Daza, 2008).

In a vision of *deveiling* pedagogies, I see Arab-Muslim feminists working to create radical possibilities and risking themselves in the far margins that bell hooks (2004) describes as sites of,

> radical possibilities, a space of resistance … a central location for the production of a counter-hegemonic discourse that is not just found in words but in habits of being and the way one lives … [it is a site that] offers to one the possibility of radical perspective from which to see and create, to imagine alternatives, new worlds. (pp. 156-157)

I see *arab-muslim* feminists looking "both from the outside in and from the inside out … [a location that provided them] "an oppositional worldview—a mode of seeing unknown to most of our oppressors" (hooks, 2004, p. 156). In other words, I see *arab-muslim* feminist researchers and teachers using their insider's literacies, organic knowledge and intuition, resilience, and deep survival skills (Delgado Bernal, 1998) to continue exposing and interrupting normative discourses, especially the *hijab* discourse.

For a vision of *deveiling* pedagogies, I call upon the community of scholars who are committed to anticolonial, antiracial and multicultural education, to reconceptualize their work with *muslim* learners as collaborative and engaging (Asher, 2002, 2003, 2007; Cammarota & Fine, 2008; Subedi & Daza, 2008). I call upon scholars to deracialize and deculturalize the conceptualization of educational studies and pedagogies (Razack, 2008). I call on the acknowledgement of subtle hybridity of *muslims* (Sirin & Fine, 2008) and the fluidity of the youth's *muslimness*. That is, instead of responding to the simplistic and confining "religious accommodations" dictated by authoritative community leaders, I call upon scholars to work with *muslim* girls in ways to enable their questionings and negotiations of the *hijab* discourse. This also includes engaging directly with young *muslims'* parents in critical and reflexive dialogues across difference (Asher, 2007). Such research and pedagogy is one that takes extended periods not only to gain a deeper understanding of the girls' lived experiences but also to build relationships of trust and solidarity with the girls and with their families in the different contexts they live.

For a vision of *deveiling* pedagogies and research, I call upon educators and researchers to persistently practice critical and strong reflexivity (Hesse-Biber & Leavy, 2007, p. 15), hybrid "release methods" (Sirin & Fine, 2008, p. 198) and "unthinkable" methodologies (Lather, 2007). It is a call for an alternative antioppressive pedagogy (Kumashiro, 2002), a "contingent, strategic, strong and vigilant" (Mirza, 2006, p. 153) pedagogy, a critically reflexive pedagogy (Asher, 2007), and an insight of love (hooks, 1994). It is a call for what Shahnaz Khan describes as "opening up of supplementary discourses" (2002, p. xx). It is a call for reflexive engagement with the unacknowledged differences (Asher, 2003, 2005, 2007; Cammarota & Fine, 2008) that may emerge between all participants who are negotiating the *hijab* as a discourse—not as a headscarf.

I also call upon researchers and educators to open spaces of for creativity and collaboration with *muslim* girls in order to, (1) navigate the multiplicity and fluidity of their subjectivities implicated by intersecting discourses in their lives, and (2) honor their choices while supporting them to negotiate the thought of as fixed Islamic values that may jeopardize their chances of any learning opportunity. This a call to work with *muslim* girls as theorizers of possibilities (Oliver & Hamzeh, 2010) and as the main agents of change in their own lives. This is a call to open with *muslim* girls opportunities to practice their agency in unpacking and challenging normative discourses in their lives, not exclusive to the *hijab* discourse (Oliver, Hamzeh, & McCaughtry, 2009). This is a call for creating a "legacy of inquiry" (Weis & Fine, 2004, pp. 98–99), a process of change that enables the disruption of normative discourse (Mirza, 2009) and opens possibilities for social justice and equity (Hamzeh, 2011). This is a call for opening spaces of struggle and uprising and cultivating moments of meaning and shifts of consciousness (Mohanty, 2003).

In a vision of *deveiling* pedagogies, I call for the cultivation of Hesse-Biber and Piatelli's "reflexive relationships" in which scholars and teachers attend to the fluidity of positions in the collective process of "crossing borders and boundaries and creating a common space for building knowledge" (2007, p. 503). This is a call to stay reflexive about "the relationship and the social [discursive] conditions that affect the conversation … we must problematize all positions whether shared or not to create a nonhierarchical environment conductive to sharing" (p. 503). This is a call to broaden the theorizing of reflexivity and validate and legitimize "the knowledge that emerges from the everyday experiences of *outsiders within* and moving subjugated knowledge *from the margin to the center* of social inquiry" (Hesse-Biber & Piatelli, 2007, p. 503). This is a call to maximize the practice of critical reflexivity in order to "bring alternative forms of knowledge into public discourse" (p. 496).

For a vision of *deveiling* pedagogies, I will constantly be channeling the calls of Layla, Dojua, Abby, and Amy,

We can tell the people how we think. (Layla)

Like there are other ways we think. (Dojua)

So people would know more about us. (Amy)

Because not everybody understands how much time it takes to get to know us, they [teachers] just need to listen more … so they appreciate us more and make more activities for girls like us … so they would know who we are and what we are so they teach us better. (Abby)

So you [teachers] appreciate us more … and can make more activities for girls our age. (Layla)

I want teachers to know that I am a teenage girl; I am just like any other girl. (Dojua)

APPENDIX A

INFORMED CONSENT FOR PARTICIPANT'S INVESTIGATIVE PROJECTS

Title of Research Project: Missing Stories of Young Muslim Girls
Principal Investigator:
Manal Hamzeh
Doctoral Student
Department of Curriculum & Instruction/College of Education
XXX University
505-xxx-xxxx

Purpose: This project is designed to learn about how adolescent Muslim girls express and negotiate the meanings of their bodily experiences in a southwestern U.S. border Muslim community. There will be four girls included in this study.

Procedures and Duration: With the researcher, Manal Hamzeh, you will be asked to write in private journals and to participate in informal conversations prompted by open-ended questions, photos they take, images they select from popular magazines, and physical activities they share, for example, wall climbing, swimming, et cetera. All interactions will be audio taped then transcribed. The activities will take place in the facilities of the Activity Center of XXXU, over 7 consecutive weeks (twice a week) beginning June 26, 2006 and until August 10, 2006. Once school starts, activities will resume for 12 consecutive weeks (once a week) from August 19 ending October 29, 2006. Each time the researcher meets with you they will spend 60-90 minutes on the research activities in Dr. Kimberly Oliver's lab area on the first floor of the Activity Center and another 60-90 minutes on

Pedagogies of Deveiling: Muslim Girls and the Hijab Discourse,
pp. 133–135
Copyright © 2012 by Information Age Publishing
133

physical activities in different spaces in the Activity Center, including the pools.

Risks: You will be under no risk while participating in this project. At all times every precaution will be taken to ensure an emotionally and physically safe environment. Any time you express to the researcher her wish to abstain from the activities of the project, you will be free to leave the circle of discussion.

Benefits of the Project: Possible benefits for you will be a better understanding of your well-being as a Muslim girl. This understanding will provide teachers with alternative insights to help them relate better to Muslim girls in general and to create more equitable educational practices.

Extent of Anonymity and Confidentiality: Your name will be anonymous. You will select a pseudonym at the beginning of the project and it will be used whenever anything is written or said. Confidentiality will be broken only when the researcher (1) knows of or suspects abuse of a girl and/or (2) believes a girl is a threat to herself or to others. At any of these times the researcher will notify the appropriate authorities. If your parent(s) requested information about you, the researcher will not disclose any data gathered in the study without your written consent.

Compensation: This project does not provide any compensation for you other than the advantage of using the facilities of the Activity Center of NMSU for the duration of the project.

Freedom to Withdraw: Your participation in this study is voluntary and withdrawal at anytime will have no consequences. You will have the choice to stop participating in the study at any time. All you need to do is to notify the researcher. You are free to not answer questions you do not wish to answer.

Approval of Research: This research has been approved, as required, by the Institutional Review Board for Research Involving Human Subjects at New Mexico University and by the Department of Curriculum and Instruction.

Participant's Responsibilities: I, _____, voluntarily agree to participate in this study.

Participant's Permission: I have read and understood the Informed Consent and conditions of this project. I have had all my questions answered. I hereby acknowledge the above and give my voluntary consent for participation in this study.

If I participate, I may withdraw ay any time without penalty. I agree to abide by the rules of this project.

_____   _____
Signature   Date

Should you have any questions about the research, please contact:

Manal Hamzeh (Principal Investigator) (505-xxx-xxxx)
Dr. Kimberly L. Oliver (Faculty Advisor) (505-xxx-xxxx)

Should you have questions about your rights as a research subject, please contact the office of the Vice President for Research at the XXX University (505-xxx-xxxx)

APPENDIX B

INFORMED CONSENT FOR PARTICIPANT'S PARENT/GUARDIAN OF INVESTIGATIVE PROJECTS

Title of Research Project: Missing Stories of Young Muslim Girls
Principal Investigator:
Manal Hamzeh
Doctoral Student
Department of Curriculum & Instruction/College of Education
XXX University
505-xxx-xxxx

Purpose: This project is designed to learn about how adolescent Muslim girls express and negotiate the meanings of their bodily experiences in a southwestern U.S. border Muslim community. There will be four girls included in this study.

Procedures and Duration: With the researcher, Manal Hamzeh, your daughter will be asked to write in private journals and to participate in informal conversations prompted by open-ended questions, photos they take, images they select from popular magazines, and physical activities they share, such as, wall climbing, swimming, et cetera. All interactions will be audio taped then transcribed. The activities will take place in the facilities of the Activity Center of XXU, in 7 consecutive weeks (twice a week) beginning June 26, 2006, and until August 10th, 2006. Once school starts, activities will resume for 12 consecutive weeks (once a week) from August 19th ending October 29th, 2006. Each time the researcher meets with the girls they will spend 60-90 minutes on the research activities in Dr. Kimberly Oliver's lab area in the first floor of the Activity Center and

Pedagogies of Deveiling: Muslim Girls and the Hijab Discourse,
pp. 137–139

another 60-90 minutes on physical activities in different spaces in the Activity Center, including the pools.

Risks: Your daughter will be under no risk while participating in this project. At all times every precaution will be taken to ensure an emotionally and physically safe environment. Any time your daughter expresses to the researcher her wish to abstain from the activities of the project, she will be free to leave the circle of discussion.

Benefits of the Project: Possible benefits for your daughter will be a better understanding of her well-being as a Muslim girl. This understanding will provide teachers with alternative insights to help them relate better to Muslim girls in general and to create more equitable educational practices.

Extent of Anonymity and Confidentiality: Your daughter's name will be anonymous. She will select a pseudonym at the beginning of the project and it will be used whenever anything is written or said confidentiality will be broken only when the researcher (1) knows of or suspects abuse of a girl and/or (2) believes a girl is a threat to herself or to others. At any of these times, the researcher will notify the appropriate authorities. If you, as a parent of a participant in this project, requested information about their daughter, the researcher will not disclose any data gathered in the study without the written consent of your daughter.

Compensation: This project does not provide any compensation for your daughter other than the advantage of using the facilities of the Activity Center of NMSU for the duration of the project.

Freedom to Withdraw: Your daughter's participation in this study is voluntary and withdrawal at anytime will have no consequences. Your daughter will have the choice to stop participating in the study at any time and all she needs to do is to notify the researcher. Your daughter is free to not answer questions she does not wish to answer.

Approval of Research: This research has been approved, as required, by the Institutional Review Board for Research Involving Human Subjects at New Mexico University and by the Department of Curriculum and instructions.

Guardian's Responsibilities: Your signature on this consent form indicates that you fully understand the above study, what is being asked of your daughter, and that you are signing it voluntarily. If you have any questions about this study, please feel free to ask them now or at any time throughout the study.

I, _____, hereby allow my daughter _____ to participate in this study.

Parent/Guardian's Permission: I have read and understood the Informed Consent and conditions of this project. I have had all my questions answered. I hereby acknowledge the above and give my agreement to allow my daughter to participate in this study.

_____   _____
Signature   Date

Should you have any questions about the research, please contact:

Manal Hamzeh (Principal Investigator) (505-xxx-xxxx)
Dr. Kimberly L. Oliver (Faculty Advisor) (505-xxx-xxxx)

Should you have questions about your rights as a research subject, please contact the office of the Vice President for Research at the XXX University (505-xxx-xxxx).

A copy of this form is for you to keep.

APPENDIX C

January 18, 2006

Mr. xxxx yyyy
Islamic Center of Al Hilal
1065 E xxx Rd.
Al Hilal, XX xxx
Phone: 505:xxx-xxxx
Email: xxxx@yahoo.com

Dear Mr. xxxx,

In reference to the two phone conversations we had last November and December, I hereby provide you in this letter with further information about my study, "Narratives of Muslim Girls." In addition, I am requesting your kind permission to conduct this study inside the women's quarters of the Islamic Center of Al Hilal.

In this study and in preparation for my doctoral dissertation, I am interested in learning about how Muslim girls experience their bodies. To do so, I will be asking all the girls to participate in conversations, open-ended interview, and journal writing, which will center on topics related to their health and physical activities provided in school or outside school (i.e., swimming, aerobics, kickboxing, gymnastics, and athletics).

The potential benefits of this study is of two fold: (1) each girl will have a better understanding of her health and well being as a Muslim girl in US public schools; and (2) knowledge gained will be used to help teachers relate better to Muslim girls with the hope of providing them with more just and equitable educational opportunities.

Pedagogies of Deveiling: Muslim Girls and the Hijab Discourse,
pp. 141–142
Copyright © 2012 by Information Age Publishing

Before beginning the project, a permission slip must be signed by the parents/guardians of each girl and the girl herself.

I hope the information provided today (see summary of the project on the second page) will facilitate your formal consideration of this study. Once you approve, please sign and return the following statement indicating consent of the research project. I am required by XXXU to have your approval prior to submitting the Institutional Review Board application.

I am looking forward to this learning opportunity with the Muslim girls in the Islamic Center of Al Jilal.

Thank you again.
With respect and trust,

Manal Hamzeh
Doctoral Student,
Curriculum & Instruction,
College of Education, XXXU
505-xxx-xxxx

As the representative of the board of the Islamic Center of Al Hilal, I approve that your study can take place on the center's premise. I will respect the confidentiality of the participants.

Name: Mr. xxxx yyyy
Signature: Date: January 18, 2006

APPENDIX D

SELF-MAPPING QUESTIONNAIRE (HELP ME KNOW YOU BETTER)

Name:
Your new/pretend name:
Age (& DOB):   Country of Birth:
School: Grade:
Plan for next year:
Today's date:
Describe yourself in terms of:
Race/Ethnicity:
Country of origin:
Culture/language(s) et cetera:

- Describe yourself/family (age/education/country of birth/first language/education/work/other):
- Who is the most important family member to you? Why?
- Who is the most important person in your life now? Why?
- Have you ever been singled out for being Muslim in school? Why?
- How did you feel and what did you do about it?
- What is the most important thing you believe in and/or do that describes you as a Muslim?
- What is your favorite thing to do and why?
- What do you like to do after school/on the weekends?
- What is your favorite public place to go to? Why?
- Who is your favorite person and/or who are your favorite people who you like to spend time with? Why?

Pedagogies of Deveiling: Muslim Girls and the Hijab Discourse,
pp. 143–144
Copyright © 2012 by Information Age Publishing

- What is your favorite physical activity? Why?
- What is your least favorite physical activity? Why?
- What do you see yourself doing/being after you graduate from high school? Why?

Date: / /

APPENDIX E

BODY COLLAGE

Pedagogies of Deveiling: Muslim Girls and the Hijab Discourse,
pp. 145

APPENDIX F

INDIVIDUAL SCRAPBOOKS

Pedagogies of Deveiling: Muslim Girls and the Hijab Discourse,
pp. 147–149
Copyright © 2012 by Information Age Publishing

APPENDIX G

TEXTUAL CONTENT OF THE FINAL BODY COLLAGE POSTER

Title: *Infinite US*
By: Abby, Amy, Dojua, and Layla

Left Shoulder: LIFE, WHUDAFXUP

Left Arm: "YYYEAH", shape, pretty smart, run, school, VIRGIN ?

Left Hand: The Risk Taker, The Cross-over (in a circle), Sagittarius-11/22 to 12/21 HERS (script under)

Right Shoulder: Strike!

Right Arm: Hip Hop, Glamour Girl, Diva, princess, obey, Aquarius 1/20 to 2/18 HERS, Pisces 2/19 to 3/20 HERS, Virgo 8/23 to 9/22 HERS, the multi-Tasker and the Dive (in circles)

Right Hand: The Award Winner and The Ingénue (in circles)

Chest: COVERGIRL, perfect, GUESS, OLAY, pleasures, Man (and right under it) HOT, MAKE A DIFFERENCE, IT'S HIPNOTIQ, beauty, TER-RORIST, LIFE, Dream, Apple Bottoms (in an apple shape), Buckle, G unit, eagle, LIVE, HU$TLA, "I'm a ROCK & ROLL TERRORIST," YOU'LL LIKE IT, TAKING BACK SUNDAY, LAGUNA

Belly up to underwear line: SHOES, girl, KORN, NUMBER ONE, Secret, Beauty, Life, LIFE, "Panic! AT THE DISCO," ROCK STAR, *DEF LEPPARD*, HUSLER, arctic Monkeys, Cosmo girl, august, Bedazzled, Power, Sephora, Bedazzled!

Under Wear Line: Property of Mike Jones

281-330-8004,

Mike Jones, Athletic Dept., Houston

Pedagogies of Deveiling: Muslim Girls and the Hijab Discourse,
pp. 151

NOTES

INTRODUCTION

1. All participants' names in this paper were pseudonyms the girls selected themselves.
2. Pseudonyms.
3. I use *arabyyah-muslimah* strategically as marker of linguistic/ethnic/racial positionalities in my scholarly/activist work. Using this term is a conscious act, which reclaims the use of my home language and *arab-muslim* histories that shaped and continue to shape my way of making sense of the world.
4. "The Arabic word *hadīth* has the primary connotation of "new," being used as antonym of *qadim*, "old." From this derived the use of the word for an item of news, a tale, a story, or a report—be it historical or legendary, true, or false ... relating to the present or to the past" (Siddiqi, 1993, p. 2). Al Hadīth "is the second scripture of Islam after the Qur'an ... serves to establish pattern (*Sunnah*) of the Prophet's life ... guiding them in their behavior and daily life.... Traditional scholars use the *Hadīth* together with the Qur'an to arrive at legal norms" (Clarke, 2003, p. 214). The Hadīth is the "prophet Muhammad's extrapolation and practice of the Qura'nic guidance also known as *Sunnah* of the Prophet" (Barazangi, 2004, p. 22). *Al Sunnah* represents the precedents and customs illustrated in the Qur'an but mostly connected to the ideal virtues and practices of Muhammad. Both the Qur'an and the *Sunnah* constitute the main sources of Islamic law (Ali, 2006). *Al Sunnah* "although originally bearing the sense of 'precedent' and 'custom' ... employed by the Muslims for accepted practice of the community, and later years, for the practice of the Prophet only" (Saddiqi, 1993, p. 2).

Pedagogies of Deveiling: Muslim Girls and the Hijab Discourse,
pp. 153–155
Copyright © 2012 by Information Age Publishing

CHAPTER 2

1. Badran writes,

   > Muslim feminist women and men engaged in gender struggle, or
   > what I have called gender activism, are (re)appropriating and reha-
   > bilitating the term in their internal struggles for gender justice. The
   > term "gender jihad" was first used by Omar Rashied, The South
   > African struggler against multiple oppressions within the community
   > and wider society, in the 1980s at the height of the antiapartheid
   > campaign that South Africans called the "Struggle." Islamic femi-
   > nists (still most often declining the label) are at once intellectuals
   > and activists—indeed, many call themselves "scholar-activists" (the
   > way secular feminists join thinking and activism or theory and prac-
   > tice)—engaging in (re)thinking or *ijtihad* (intellectual struggle to
   > understand) and *jihad* (activist struggle). The connectedness of *ijti-
   > had* and *jihad* is expressed in the fact that the two words come from
   > the same Arabic root. (2008, p. 311).

2. A.H. marks the years after the *Hijrah*, the immigration of Mohammed and
   his followers from Mecca to Al Medina. That is, A.D. 622 constitutes the
   first year of the Muslim calender.
3. Mecca, the city, is valued by Muslims for having the holiest site of Islam, Al
   Masjid Al Haram.
4. All translated Qur'anic verses are retrieved from Yusuf (2002).
5. All original Arabic Qur'anic verses are retrieved from *Al Qur'an Al Kareem*
   edition of *Majma' Al Malek Fahed* for printing the Holy Qur'an—a gift from
   my friend Youef Arouri brought from Al Medinah on his 2009 *'Umra* trip.
6. Sharia or *shari'a*

   > means a pathway.... It is not a narrow pathway, but rather a broad
   > pathway. It is defined by individual tracks that converge and diverge
   > as the sheep make their way, adjusting to local terrain, some moving
   > in large clusters and others wandering in exploratory forays or ven-
   > turing alone along previously uncharted courses ... the *shari'a* as
   > Islamic law allows for diversity and is based upon difference of opin-
   > ion within the limits of shared sources and principles. (Kugle, 2010,
   > p. 133)

7. Sahih Al Bukhari, volume 7, book 67 (*Al Nikah*), ch. 68, *hadīth* 5166, pp.
   72-73. (All cited *ahadīth* are retrieved from Khan (1997).
8. Sahih Al Bukhari, volume 9, book 93 (*Al Fitan*), ch. 18, *hadīth* 7099, p. 145.
9. "Arabic *hadīth*" or "The Prophet said: 'After me I have not left any *Fitnah*
   (trial and affliction) more harmful to men than women.'" (Sahih Al
   Bukhari, volume 7, book 67 (Al Nikah), chapter 18, *hadīth* 5096, p. 35).
10. It is also worth noting that the Prophet had asked His Companions not to
    record anything but the Qur'an, "the Prophet said, 'Do not write down

anything from me except the Qur'an. He who has noted down anything from me apart from the Qur'an must erase it'" (Kugle, 2010, p. 284).

CHAPTER 4

1. Hamzeh is the name of the Prophet's uncle.
2. Jordan's majority population is Muslim.
3. *Mu'athen* (Arabic, noun) the person designated with the responsibility of calling for prayer from the minaret of a mosque.
4. *Ifttar* is the after sunset meal in which a Muslim breaks his/her daylong fast.
5. To Muslims alcohol is one of the common forbidden—*haram*—substances. Some Muslims believe that they are explicitly forbidden to approach alcohol, that is, not to trade, consume, handle, or be in close physical proximity to it. Others believe they are not allowed to pray while drunk.

CHAPTER 5

1. The *jilbab* is the loose, long, shapeless jacket worn over regular clothes in public.

GLOSSARY OF ARABIC TERMS

Al Bukhari or Muhammad ibn Ismail Al Bukhari (194–256 A.H.) is the Persian Muslim scholar who collected and authenticated the *ahadīth* in his book, which came to be known as Sahih Al Bukhari.

al hareem. What/who a man protects such as a woman who is only allowed to be with her husband and is forbidden for any other man.

Al Hilal. The crescent.

Al Hijrah. The immigration of Mohammed and his followers from Mecca to Al Medina in A.D. 622.

al hishma. The virtue by which a Muslim maintains her/his moderation, humility, and respect—derived from the Arabic root *hshm*, to anger and to cause embarrassment (*Lisan Al 'Arab*).

al hurmah. What/who is not allowed to be violated or not allowed to be permissible.

Al Jiser. The bridge.

Al Tabari or Abu Ja'far Muhammad ibn Jarir al-Tabari (224–310 A.H.), is the Mulsim prominent and independent *ijtihad* scholar and historian, who wrote the extensive interpretation of the Qura'n in *Tafsir Al Tabari.*

akkinnah. Veils.

arabyyah-muslimah. Feminine form of the term Arab-Muslim.

Asbab al nuzul. The reasons of revelations.

'asr. Afternoon or afternoon prayer.

ayyat. Qur'anic verses of each chapter (*surah*).

da'if. Weak or defective *hadīth*.

Pedagogies of Deveiling: Muslim Girls and the Hijab Discourse,
pp. 157–159
Copyright © 2012 by Information Age Publishing

Dhuhr. Noon and noon prayers.

dhulumat. Darkness or veils/covers causing darkness.

Falah. Attaining/gaining Paradise, prosperity, or victory (*Lisan Al 'Arab*). Derived from the Arabic root *flh.*

Fiqh. Deep understandings or the "major collection of the jurisprudential interpretations of the Qur'an and jurisprudential rulings based on the Hadīth.

Fitnah. It is the noun that is derived from the Arabic root *ftn,* to burn, kill, and fight, have a difference in opinion, or tempt or seduce (*Lisan Al 'Arab*).

ghishyyah. Veil.

ghita'. Veil.

hadīth. The primary connotation of "new," being used as antonym of *qadim,* "old." From this derived the use of the word for an item of news, a tale, a story, or a report—be it historical or legendary, true, or false … relating to the present or to the past" (Saddiqi, 1993, p. 2). Al Hadīth "is the second scripture of Islam after the Qur'an … serves to establish pattern (*Sunnah*) of the Prophet's life … guiding them in their behaviour and daily life…. Traditional scholars use the Hadīth together with the Qur'an to arrive at legal norms" (Clarke, 2003, p. 214). The Hadīth is the "prophet Muhammad's extrapolation and practice of the Qura'nic guidance also known as *Sunnah* of the Prophet" (Barazangi, 2004, p. 22). Al Sunnah represents the precedents and customs illustrated in the Qur'an but mostly connected to the ideal virtues and practices of Muhammad. Both the Qur'an and the *Sunnah* constitute the main sources of Islamic law (Ali, 2006). *Al Sunnah* "although originally bearing the sense of 'precedent' and 'custom' … employed by the Muslims for accepted practice of the community, and later years, for the practice of the Prophet only" (Saddiqi, 1993, p. 2).

halal. Permissible (*Lisan Al 'Arab*).

haram. It is the noun derived from the verb *hrm.* It is what is made sacred and safe like the premise of the mosque or one's private space. The most common use of the term *haram* applies to certain forbidden practices such as eating pork, drinking alcohol, using drugs, socializing in coed spaces. *Haram* is the opposite of what it allowed, *halal,* permissible (*Lisan Al 'Arab*).

hasan. Good enough *hadīth.*

hijab. The noun *hijab* is derived from the Arabic root *hjb,* to hide, guard, prevent, and establish a border or screen (*Lisan Al 'Arab*), then the *hijab* is according to *arab-muslim* feminist Fatima Mernissi (1991) multidimensional—visual, spatial, ethical, and spiritual (1991).

Hijabah. The sacred cover of the shrine of *Ka'ba in* Mecca and the curtain separating the caliph from the members of his court (Mernissi, 1991).

Ifttar. The after sunset meal in which a Muslim breaks his/her day-long fast.

inshallah. God willing.

imam. The leader of a group prayer.

ijihad. Engaging in (re)thinking or intellectual struggle to understand.

isnad. The method of establishing the reliability of the oral reporting of a *hadīth* or authenticating the transmission chain of a *hadīth*.

jalābībihinna. Cloaks used by women (*jilbab*, singular form of *jilbabs* or *jalābībihinna*).

Jihad. Activist struggle. *ijtihad* and *jihad* are derived from the same Arabic root *jhd*.

jilbab. Loose long shapeless jacket worn in public over regular clothes.

Ka'ba. The black cube shaped shrine in the main mosque, Masjid Al Haram, in Mecca. Muslims walk around it during the pilgrimage rituals and orient themselves towards it during prayers.

khumrīhinna. Face covers used by women.

Lisan Al 'Arab. The Tongue or Language of the Arabs (a major Arabic dictionary).

mahjoob. The covered thing or person.

maqbul. Acceptable *hadīth*.

mardud. Rejected *hadīth*.

masslah al nisa'. Women prayer's area.

matn. The method of validating the content of a *hadīth*. It is secondary to *isnad*.

mawdu'. Fabricated *hadīth* .

mu'athen. The person who calls for prayer from the minaret of a mosque.

mushtabah. Suspected *hadīth*.

muslimat. The plural of *muslimah*, or *muslim* female.

Mutawatir. The *hadīth* that is authenticate due its continuous reporting.

Qiyas. Analogical reasoning.

Quraysh. The Meccan tribe of the Prophet Muhammad.

Sitr. A curtain.

ta'arrud. To accost, stand in the way and harass.

Tafsir. The major classical methodology of Islamic exegesis.

zina. Sexual activities outside heterosexual marriage.

REFERENCES

Abu El Fadl, K. (2001). *Speaking in God's name: Islamic law, authority and women.* Oxford, England: Oneworld.

Ahmed, L. (1992). *Women and gender in Islam: Historical roots of a modern debate.* New Haven, CT: Yale University Press.

Ahmed, S. (2002). Racialized bodies. In M. Evans & E. Lee (Eds.), *Real bodies: A sociological introduction* (pp. 46-63). New York, NY: Palgrave.

Ali, K. (2006). *Sexual ethics and Islam: Feminist reflection on Qur'an, hadith, and jurisprudence.* Oxford, England: Oneword.

Anzaldúa, G. (1987). *Borderlands/la frontera: The new mestizas.* San Francisco, CA: Aunt Lute Books.

Asher, N. (2002). (En)gendering a hybrid consciousness. *Journal of Curriculum Theorizing, 18*(4),81-92.

Asher, N. (2003). Engaging difference: Towards a pedagogy of interbeing. *Teaching Education, 14*(3), 236-247.

Asher, N. (2005). Engaging postcolonial and feminist perspectives for a multicultural education pedagogy in the south. *Teachers College Record, 107*(5), 1079-1106.

Asher, N. (2007). Made in the (multicultural) U.S.A.: Unpacking tensions of race, culture, gender, and sexuality in education. *Educational Researcher, 36*(2), 65-73.

Azzarito, L., & Solmon, M. A. (2005). A reconceptualization of physical education: The intersection of gender/race/social class. *Sport, Education and Society, 10*(1), 25-47.

Azzarito, L., Solmon, M. A., & Harrison, L. (2006). "… If I had a choice, I would …": A feminist post-structuralist perspective on girls in physical education. *Research Quarterly for Exercise and Sport, 77*(2), 222-239.

Badran, M. (1985). Islam, patriarchy, and feminism in the Middle East. *Trends in History, 4*(1), 49-71.

Badran, M. (1995). *Feminists, Islam, and nation: Gender and the making of Modern Egypt.* Princeton, NJ: Princeton University Press.

Badran, M. (2009). *Feminism in Islam secular and religious convergences.* Oxford, England: Oneworld.

Badran, M. (2009). *Feminism in Islam secular and religious convergences.* Oxford, England: Oneworld.

Barazangi, N. H. (2004). *Women identity and the Qur'an: A new reading.* Gainsville, FL: University Press of Florida.

Barazangi, N. H. (2009). The absence of Muslim women shaping Islamic thought: Foundations of Muslims' peaceful and just co-existance. *Journal of Law and Religion, 24*(403), 101-130.

Basit, T. N. (1997). "I want more freedom, but not too much": British Muslim girls and the dynamism of family values. *Gender 7 Education, 9*(4), 425-440.

Benn, T. (1996). Muslim women and physical education in initial teacher training. *Sport, Education and Society, 1*(1), 5-21.

Benn, T. (2000a). Towards inclusion in education and physical education. In A. Williams (Ed.), *Primary school physical education, research into practice* (pp. 118-135). London, England: Routledge.

Benn, T. (2000b). Valuing cultural diversity: the challenge for physical education. In S. Capel & S. Piotrowski (Eds.), *Issues in physical education* (pp. 64-78). London, England: Routledge.

Benn, T. (2002) Muslim women in teacher training: issues of gender, 'race' and religion. In D. Penney (Ed.), *Gender and physical education* (pp. 57-79). London, England: Routledge.

Bordo, S. (1993). *Unbearable weight: Feminism, Western culture, and the body.* Berkeley, CA: University of California Press.

Benn, T., & Dagkas, S. (2006). Incompatible? Compulsory mixed-sex physical education initial teacher training (PEITT) and the inclusion of Muslim women: a case-study on seeking solutions. *European Physical Education Review, 12*(2), 181-200.

Brown, L., & Strega, S. (Ed.) (2005). *Research as resistance: Critical, indigenous and anti-oppressive approaches.* Toronto, Ontario, Canada: Canadian Scholars' Press.

Butler, J. (1990). *Gender trouble.* New York, NY: Routledge.

Cammarota, J., & Fine, M. (2008). *Revolutionizing education: Youth participatory action research in motion.* New York, NY: Routledge.

Clandinin, D. (Ed.) (2007). *Handbook of narrative inquiry: Mapping a methodology.* Thousand Oaks, CA: SAGE.

Clarke, L. (2003). *Hijab* according to the *hadīth*: Text and interpretation. In S. S. Alvi, H. Hoodfar, & S. McDonough (Eds.), *The Muslim veil in North America: Issues and debates* (pp. 214-286). Toronto, Ontario, Canada: Women's Press.

Cortis, N., Sawrikar, P., & Muir, K. (2007). Participation in sport and recreation by culturally and linguistically diverse women. *Social Policy Research Centre Report, 4*, i-vi, 1-46. University of New South Wales.

Craig, J. C., & Huber, J. (2007). Relational reverberation. In D. J. Clandinin (Ed.), *Handbook of narrative inquiry: Mapping a methodology* (pp. 251-279). Thousand Oaks, CA: SAGE.

Dagkas, S., & Benn, T. (2006). Young Muslim women's experiences of Islam and physical education in Greece and Britain: A comparative study. *Sport, Education and Society, 11*(1), 21-38.

Davies, B. (2000). *A body of writing, 1990–1999.* New York, NY: AltaMira Press.

De Knop, P., Theeboom, M., Wittock, H., & De Martelaer, K. (1996). Implications of Islam on Muslim girls' sport participation in Western Europe. Literature and policy recommendations for sport promotion. *Sport, Education, and Society, 1*(2), 147-164.

Delgado Bernal, D. (1998). Using a Chicana feminist epistemology in educational research. *Harvard Educational Review, 68,* 555-582.

Denzin, N. K., & Lincoln, Y. S. (Eds.). (2005). *The SAGE handbook of qualitative research* (3rd ed.). Thousand Oaks, CA: SAGE.

El Guindi, F. (1999). *Veil: Modesty, privacy, and resistance.* Oxford, England: Berg.

Elnour, A., & Bashir-Ali, K. (2003). Teaching Muslim girls in American schools. *Social Education, 67*(1), 62-66.

El Saadawi, N. (1998). *The Nawal Al Saadawi reader.* New York, NY: Zed Books.

Fine, M. (2004). Foreword: All about the girl. In A. Harris (Ed.), *All about the girl: Culture, power, and identity* (pp. xi-xv). New York, NY: Routledge.

Fine, M. (2007). Feminist designs for difference. In S. N. Hesse-Biber (Ed.), *Handbook of feminist research: Theory and praxis.* Thousand Oaks: CA: SAGE.

Fine, M., & McClelland, S. I. (2007). The politics of teen women's sexuality: Public policy and the adolescent female body. Equality and Reproductive Rights Symposium, Center for Reproductive Rights. *Emory Law Journal, 56*(4), 995-1038.

Flintoff, A., & Scraton, S. (2001). Stepping into active leisure? Young women's perceptions of active lifestyles and their experiences of school physical education. *Sport, Education & Society, 6*(1), 5-21.

Gannon, S., & Davies, B. (2007). Postmodern, poststructural, and critical theories. In S. H Hesse-Biber (Ed.). *Handbook of feminist research: Theory & praxis* (pp. 71-106). Thousand Oaks: CA: SAGE.

Giroux, H. (2001). *Theory and resistance in education: A pedagogy for the opposition.* Westport, CT: Bergin & Garvey.

Greene, M. (1995). *Releasing the imagination: Essays on education, the arts, and social change.* San Francisco, CA: Jossey-Bass.

Hamdan, A. (2007). The issue of the Hijab in France: Reflections and analysis. *Muslim World Journal of Human Rights, 4*(2), 1079-1079.

Hamzeh Al Smadi, M. (2007). *A de-veiling narrative inquiry: Entry and agency in body stories of Muslim girls* (Doctoral dissertation). Retrieved from ProQuest Digital Dissertations & Theses. (AAT 3383028)

Hamzeh, M. (in press). Deveiling body stories: Muslim girls negotiate visual, spatial, and ethical *hijabs. Race, Ethnicity & Education.*

Hamzeh, M., & Oliver, K. (2010). Gaining research access into the lives of Muslim girls: Researchers negotiating muslimness, modesty, *inshallah,* and *haram. International Journal of Qualitative Studies in Education, 23*(2), 165-180.

Hargreaves, J. (2007). Sport, exercise, and the female Muslim body: Negotiating Islam, politics, and the male power. In J. Hargreaves & P. Vertinsky (Eds.), *Physical culture, power and the body* (pp. 74-100). New York, NY: Routledge.

Harris, A. (2004). *Future girl: Young women in the twenty-first century.* New York, NY: Routledge.

Herschmann, N. J. (2004). Feminist standpoint as postmodern strategy. In S. Harding (Ed.), *The feminist standpoint theory reader: Intellectual & political controversies* (pp. 317-332). New York, NY: Routledge.

Hesse-Biber, S. N., & Brooks, A. (2007). Core feminist insights and strategies on authority, representations, truths, reflexivity, and ethics across the research process. In S. N. Hesse-Biber (Ed.), *Handbook of feminist research: Theory and praxis* (pp. 419-424). Thousand Oaks, CA: SAGE.

Hesse-Biber, S. N., & Leavy, P. (2006). *The practice of qualitative research*. Thousand Oaks, CA: SAGE.

Hesse-Biber, S. N., & Leavy, P. (2007). *Feminist research practice: A primer*. Thousand Oaks, CA: SAGE.

Hesse-Biber, S. N., & Piatelli, D. (2007). Holistic reflexivity: The feminist practice of reflexivity. In S. N. Hesse-Biber (Ed.), *Handbook of feminist research: Theory and praxis* (pp. 493-514). Thousand Oaks, CA: SAGE.

Hill-Collins, P. (1990). *Black feminist thought: Knowledge, consciousness, and the politics of empowerment*. New York, NY: Routledge.

Hill-Collins, P. (2004). Learning from the outsider within: The sociological significance of Black feminist thought. In S. Harding (Ed.). *The feminist standpoint theory reader: Intellectual & political controversies* (pp. 103-126). New York, NY: Routledge.

hooks, b. (1994). *Teaching to transgress: Education as the practice of freedom*. New York, NY: Routledge.

hooks, b. (2004). Choosing the margin as a space of radical openness. In S. Harding (Ed.), *The feminist standpoint theory reader: Intellectual & political controversies* (pp. 153-159). New York, NY: Routledge.

Josselson, R. (2007). The ethical attitude in narrative research: Principles and practicalities. In D. J. Clandinin (Ed.), *Handbook of narrative inquiry: Mapping a methodology* (pp. 537-566). Thousand Oaks, CA: SAGE.

Kahan, D. (2003). Islam and physical activity: Implications for American sport and physical educators. *The Journal of Physical Education, Recreation & Dance, 74*(3), 48-54.

Keaton, T. D. (2006). *Muslim girls and the other France: Race, identity politics, & social exclusion*. Bloomington, IN: Indiana University Press.

Khan, S. (2002). *Aversion and desire: Negotiating Muslim female identity in the diaspora*. Toronto, Ontario, Canada: Women's Press.

Khan, M. M. (1997). *Al Bukhari, Sahih: Translation of the meanings of Arabic-English*. Riyadh, Saudi Arabia: Dara Al Salam.

Kincheloe, J. L., Steinberg, S. R., & Stonebank, C. D. (2010). *Teaching against Islamophobia*. New York, NY: Peter Lang

Kugle, S. A. (2010). *Homosexuality in Islam: Critical reflection on gay, lesbian, and transgender Muslims*. Oxford, England: Oneworld.

Kumashiro, K. (2002). *Troubling education: Queer activism and antioppressive pedagogy*. New York, NY: RoutlegeFalmer.

Lather, P. (1986). Issues of validity in openly ideological research: Between a rock and soft place. *Interchange, 17*(4), 63-84.

Lather, P. (2007). *Getting lost: Feminist efforts toward a double(d) science*. New York, NY: State University of New York Press.

Lieblich, A. (2006). Vicissitudes. *Qualitative Inquiry, 20*(10), 1-21.

Lieblich, A., Tuval-Mashiach, R., & Zilber, T. (1998). *Narrative research: Reading, analysis, and interpretation.* Thousand Oaks: SAGE.

Limage, L. J. 2000. Education and Muslim identity: The case of France. *Comparative Education, 36*(1), 73-94.

Lisan Al 'Arab (Arabic Dictionary). Retrieved from Al Baheth Al Arabi website: http://www.baheth.info/

Mahmood, S. (2005). *Politics of piety: The Islamic revival and the feminist subject.* Princeton, NJ: Princeton University Press.

Martin, J. J., McCaughtry, N., & Shen, B. (2008). Predicting physical activity in Arab American school children. *Journal of Teaching in Physical Education, 27*(2), 205-219.

Mashhour, A. (2005). Islamic law and gender equality: Could there be a common ground?: A study of divorce and polygamy in Sharia law and contemporary legislation in Tunisia and Egypt. *Human Rights Quarterly, 27*(2), 562-596.

Maxwell, J. A. (1996). *Qualitative research design: An interactive approach.* Thousand Oaks, CA: SAGE.

Meetoo, V., & Mirza, H. M. (2007). "There is nothing 'honourable' about honour killings": Gender violence and the limits of multiculturalism. *Women's Studies International Forum, 30*(3), 187-200.

Mernissi, F. (1991). *The veil and the male elite: A feminist interpretation of women's rights in Islam* (M. J. Lakeland, Trans.). Cambridge, MA: Perseus Books.

Mirza, H. S. (2006). 'Race', gender and educational desire. *Race Ethnicity and Education, 9*(2), 137-58.

Mirza, H. S. (2009). Plotting a history: Black and postcolonial feminisms in 'new times.' *Race Ethnicity and Education, 12*(1), 1-10.

Mohanty, C. T. (2003). *Feminism without borders: Decolonizing theory, practicing solidarity.* Durham, NC: Duke University.

Oliver, K. L. (2003). Images of the body from popular culture: Engaging adolescent girls in critical inquiry. In L. Sander-Bustle (Ed.), *Image, inquiry, and transformative practice: Engaging learners in creative and critical inquiry through visual representation* (pp. 51-85). New York, NY: Peter Lang.

Oliver, K. L., & Hamzeh, M. (2010). "The boys won't let us play": 5th grade *mestizas* publicly challenge physical activity discourse at school. *Research Quarterly for Exercise and Sport, 81*(1), 39-51.

Oliver. K. L., Hamzeh, M., & McCaughtry, N. (2009). Girly girls can play games "Las niñas pueden jugar tambien": 5th grade girls negotiate self-identified barriers to physical activity. *Journal of Teaching in Physical Education, 28*(1), 90-110.

Oliver, K., & Lalik, R. M. (2000). *Bodily knowledge: Learning about equity & justice with adolescent girls.* New York, NY: Peter Lang.

Pfister, G. (2000). Doing sport in a headscarf: German sport and Turkish females. *Journal of Sport History, 27*(3), 497-524.

Razack, S. (2008). *Casting out: The eviction of Muslims from Western laws & politics.* Toronto, Ontario: University of Toronto Press.

Reay, D. (2007). Future directions in difference research: Recognizing and responding to difference. In S. N. Hesse-Biber (Ed.), *Handbook of feminist research: Theory and praxis* (pp. 605-612). Thousand Oaks: SAGE.

Said, E. W. (1979). *Orientalism*. New York, NY: Vintage Books.

Sandoval, C. (2000). *Methodology of the oppressed*. Minneapolis, MN: University of Minnesota Press.

Sarroub, L. (2001). The sojourner experience of Yemeni American high school students: An ethnographic portrait. *Harvard Educational Review, 71*(3), 390-415.

Shapiro, S., & Shapiro, S., (Eds.). (2002). *Body movements: Pedagogy, politics, & social change*. Cresskill, NJ: Hampton Press.

Sirin, S. R., & Fine, M. (2008). *Muslim American youth: Understanding hyphenated identities through multiple methods*. New York, NY: New York University Press.

Strandbu, A. (2005). Identity, embodied culture and physical exercise: Stories from Muslim girls in Oslo with immigrant background. *Nordic Journal of Youth Research, 13*(1), 27-45.

Subedi, B., & Daza, S. L. (2008). The possibilities of postcolonial praxis in education. *Race Ethnicity and Education, 11*(1), 1-10.

Swar, A. L., & Nagar, R. (2010). *Critical transnational feminist praxis*. Albany, NY: SUNY Press.

Subedi, B., & Daza, S. L. (2008). The possibilities of postcolonial praxis in education. *Race Ethnicity and Education, 11*(1), 1-10.

Thomas, R. (2005). Honouring the oral traditions of my ancestors through story telling. In L. Brown & S. Strega (Eds.), *Research as resistance: Critical, indigenous and anti-oppressive approaches* (pp. 237-254). Toronto, Ontario, Canada: Canadian Scholars' Press.

Wadud, A. (1999). *Qur'an and women: Rereading of the sacred text from women's prespective*. Oxford, England: Oxford University Press.

Walseth, K. (2006). Young Muslim women & sport: The impact of identity work. *Leisure Studies, 25*(1), 75-94.

Walseth, K., & Fasting, K. (2003). Islam's view on physical activity and sport: Egyptian women interpreting Islam. *International Review for the Sociology of Sport, 38*(1), 45-60.

Weedon, C. (1997). *Feminist practice & poststructuralist theory*. Malden, MA: Blackwell.

Weedon, C. (1999). *Feminism, theory and the politics of difference*. Malden, MA: Blackwell.

Weis, L., & Fine, M. (2004). *Working methods: Research and social justice*. New York, NY: Routledge.

Windle, J. (2004). Schooling, symbolism and social power: The Hijab in Republican France. *The Australian Educational Researcher, 31*(1), 95-112.

Yusf, A. A. (2002). *The holy Qur'an: Text, translation and commentary*. Elmhurst, NY: Tahrike Tarsile Qur'an.

Zaman, H. (1997). Islam, well-being, and physical activity: Perceptions of Muslim young women. In G. Clarke & B. Humberstone (Eds.), *Researching women and sport* (pp. 50-67). Hampshire, England: Palgrave Macmillan.

Zine, J. (2003). Dealing with September 12: Integrative antiracism and the challenge of anti-Islamophobia education. *Orbit, 33*(3), 39-41.

Zine, J. (2004). Anti-Islamophobia education as transformative pedagogy: Reflections from the educational front lines. *The American Journal of Islamic Social Sciences, 21*(3), 110-119.

Zine, J. (2006a). Unveiled sentiments: gendered Islamophobia and experiences of veiling among Muslim girls in a Canadian Islamic School. *Equity & Excellence in Education, 39*(3), 239-52.

Zine, J. (2006b). Between orientalism and fundamentals: The politics of Muslim women's feminist engagement. *Muslim World Journal of Human Rights, 3*(1), 1-24.

Zine, J. (2007). Safe havens or religious 'ghettos'? Narratives of Islamic schooling in Canada. *Race Ethnicity and Education, 10*(1), 71-92.

ABOUT THE AUTHOR

Manal Hamzeh is an assistant professor in the Department of Sociology and Women's Studies of New Mexico State University (NMSU). She holds a PhD in curriculum and instruction from NMSU. As an *arabyyah/muslimah* in *exile,* her research is guided by *arab-muslim* feminisms and feminist postcolonial theories to critically interrogate gendering discourses in the lives *muslim* girls. Her work has been published in *International Journal of Qualitative Studies in Education,* the *Journal of Race, Ethnicity & Education, Research Quarterly for Exercise and Sport,* and *Journal of Teaching in Physical Education.*

INDEX

CPSIA information can be obtained at www.ICGtesting.com
Printed in the USA
BVOW010612220113

311222BV00004B/62/P